DEFENDING THE FREE MARKET

PRAISE FOR

DEFENDING THE FREE MARKET

"I've been eagerly anticipating such a book from Father Sirico for a long time. The man has delivered magnificently. *Defending the Free Market* does more than the title suggests. It celebrates the miracle of freedom and points a lost generation back to the free and virtuous society."

—Lawrence Kudlow,
anchor of CNBC's The Kudlow Report

"Father Robert Sirico is a voice who must be heard. *Defending the Free Market* provides a solidly Christian perspective on capitalism and free markets—and makes the compelling case that we cannot possibly understand economics and how markets function without understanding the true nature of man."

—Chuck Colson,
founder of Prison Fellowship® and the Colson Center for Christian Worldview

"*Defending the Free Market* addresses the morality of entrepreneurship from the point of view of a sophisticated economist who is also an inspiring theologian, leading us on a journey to the free and virtuous society, animated by human creativity in the image of the Creator."

—George Gilder,
author of Wealth and Poverty

"As Father Sirico so rightly points out, no other system in history has lifted more people out of abject poverty than capitalism, but capitalism without a moral compass leads to a system and a society lost in the wilderness. *Defending the Free Market* reminds us of the moral responsibility of freedom and provides the perspective to see beyond our immediate goals and desires into the type of future we envision for our children and our nation."

—Dave Van Andel,
chairman and CEO of the Van Andel Institute

"If you think 'something in our world is distracted, disordered, out of joint,' read Father Robert Sirico's new book. It is well worth the journey."

—William E. LaMothe,
retired chairman and CEO of Kellogg Company

"Refreshing, uplifting, and encouraging, Father Robert Sirico understands how human beings can succeed in life, both economically and spiritually, and offers clear answers to the arguments against people's ability to take destiny into their own hands. *Defending the Free Market* is required reading for the current and next generation of leaders."

—Dr. Juan Jose Daboub,
former managing director of the World Bank

"Father Robert Sirico is an evangelist for freedom. For more than twenty years he has persuasively explained the value of economic freedom in helping the poor become productive, creative, and virtuous. And he has expanded the free exchange of economic ideas in theological circles, demonstrating that the Christian tradition and economic ideas can enrich each other. This book advances that important argument."

—Father Raymond J. de Souza,
columnist for Canada's National Post

"My brother, Father Robert, says what he means and means what he says. This is a wonderful book!"

—Tony Sirico,
film and television actor who played Paulie Gualtieri on The Sopranos

"Father Sirico's Acton Institute has helped change the way peoples around the world think of liberty. And the opening passages in his new book grab your attention and don't let go. The rest of the book keeps the promise made in the beginning. His explanations for key terms are unusually clear. The central word in his text is 'UNLESS...'"

—Michael Novak,
former U.S. ambassador to the U.N. Human Rights Commission

"Every American concerned about our economy and the erosion of individual liberty should read Father Sirico's insightful and well-reasoned book. As he makes crystal clear, our prosperity will continue to be provided not by government but through the proven power of the economic and personal freedoms we enjoy within American free enterprise."

—Rich DeVos,
co-founder of Amway and chairman of the Orlando Magic

DEFENDING THE FREE MARKET

THE MORAL CASE *for a* FREE ECONOMY

THE REV. ROBERT SIRICO

Cataloging-in-Publication data on file with the Library of Congress
ISBN 978-1-59698-325-0

Published in the United States by
Regnery Publishing, Inc.
One Massachusetts Avenue NW
Washington, DC 20001
www.Regnery.com

Manufactured in the United States of America
10 9 8 7 6 5 4 3 2 1

Books are available in quantity for promotional or premium use. Write to Director of Special Sales, Regnery Publishing, Inc., One Massachusetts Avenue NW, Washington, DC 20001, for information on discounts and terms or call (202) 216-0600.

Distributed to the trade by
Perseus Distribution
387 Park Avenue South
New York, NY 10016

For

Kris Alan Mauren

Sirach 6:14–17

Contents

vulnerable to simply being outcompeted by the more industrious in an increasingly global labor market.

Then, too, consider the breakdown of trust, integrity, and responsible freedom that contributed mightily to the continuing financial crisis, which began in 2008.

All of these trends have one thing in common—a selfish failure to look beyond our own lives. The attitude is perfectly summed up in the words of the economist whose misguided theories have done so much to steer many nations into bankruptcy. John Maynard Keynes said, "In the long run we are all dead." In that single sentence he captured everything that was missing from his economic worldview and much of what's wrong with America and the world today.

Too many of us have lost hope. We may expect to have fun tomorrow or over the upcoming weekend. But a more richly imagined hope—one whereby we project and pledge ourselves to a future characterized by human flourishing for ourselves and future generations, for our communities and the nation—this, I suggest, has been eroded over the past fifty years and replaced with a vision of ourselves as without a destiny and calling, without a worthy purpose.

The problem isn't just a numbers game, and it can't be solved by simply tweaking this or that budget line, or wringing a little waste out of the system here or there. What threatens to bring freedom to an end is that we have forgotten the end of freedom, in the other sense—its aim or purpose.

The confusion is all around us. Liberty is confused with license, cronyism with capitalism, mere schooling with education, Social Security with genuine intergenerational solidarity, and real social responsibility with taking money from one group and giving it to another—and never mind the cultural devastation wrought upon the recipients by this Orwellian form of "welfare." We have come to believe that the government bureaucrat is a Good Samaritan.

All too many confuse a market economy with consumerism, seeing a buy-buy-buy mentality as the outcome and goal of economic liberty. But consumerism is the muddled idea that only in *having* more can we *be* more. Rather than the Cartesian formulation, "*cogito ergo sum*" ("I think therefore I am"), some have come to believe that shopping is the proof of existence: "*consumo ergo sum.*" Consumerism is wrong not because material things are wrong. Consumerism is wrong because it worships what is beneath us.

Far from a synonym for capitalism, consumerism makes capitalism impossible over the long term, since it makes capital formation all but impossible. A consumer culture isn't a saving culture, isn't a thrift culture. It's too fixated on buying the next toy to ever delay gratification, to ever save and invest for the future. The point is elementary: you can't have sustainable capitalism without capital; you can't have capital without savings; and you can't save if you're running around spending everything you've just earned. But the confusion has grown so deep that many people today do not have the ears to hear it. Indeed, the policies of our nation's central bank seem to reinforce this habit by driving down interest rates to near zero and thereby denying people a material reward—in the form of interest on their banked savings—for foregoing consumption.

Can it be mere coincidence that we are beset by decline just as the Judeo-Christian worldview has retreated from the public square? We are suffering a crisis of confidence whereby no one can judge any idea, person or culture without in turn being judged an absolutist or hatemonger. The idea seems to be that all worldviews can come together on the allegedly neutral ground of secular relativism and "all just get along." The loudest proponents of tolerance have become the most intolerant, and they don't even seem to notice the contradiction. Meanwhile, many of the rest of us seem to have forgotten that secular relativists have a worldview of their own. We've appointed them—who are really our fellow contestants—referees in the cultural contest of ideas, and then we sit and wonder why our country appears to have lost the animating moral logic that once sustained it.

When the Judeo-Christian worldview is replaced by a vaguely formed and only partially acknowledged philosophical materialism, then all that matters is what we can get for ourselves today. What is lost is a sense of history as a meaningful and linear thing, as something moving toward a great consummation. When a person loses that, when a whole people loses that, when the institutions that serve to organize and govern a people lose that, the loss is severe and reverberating.

When freedom is divorced from faith, both freedom and faith suffer. Freedom becomes rudderless, because truth gives freedom its direction. The most adept political player with the flashiest new policy or program can lead the people around by the nose. Freedom without a moral orientation has no guiding star. On the other hand, when a people surrenders their freedom to the government—the freedom to make moral, economic, religious, and social choices and then take personal responsibility for the consequences—virtue tends to waste away and faith itself grows cold. Theocracy is the destruction of human freedom in the name of God. Libertinism is the destruction of moral norms in the name of liberty. Neither will do.

The link between economic liberty and public morality is not tenuous; it is clear and direct. Economic liberty exists where private property and the rule of law are respected. Consider the case of modern Russia, a culture of rich and poor with only a small and struggling middle class—because corruption is rampant in its pseudo-market institutions. While a few friends of the government higher-ups make out like gangbusters, the vast majority of the population, including the class of poor but aspiring entrepreneurs, often finds itself facing an unscalable wall of insider cronyism.

Or to take the flip side of this pattern, history shows that societies with a consistent respect for the sanctity of private property and other economic rights also tend to have relatively intact cultures, along with rising standards of living not just for the wealthy but also for the middle class and the poor.

One word of warning: as soon as we begin talking about rights, we have to be very clear what we mean, since a lot of mischief against human freedom has been committed in the name of so-called "rights." The moral defense of liberty requires that we make distinctions between rights and privileges, between society and government, between community and the collective. Rights, society, and community are all part of the natural order of liberty. Privileges, government, and the collective are not entirely separate, but they are essentially different in that they rest on coercion.

A moral argument for economic liberty should not shrink from its own logical implications, however politically unfashionable they may be. The imperative against theft and in favor of the security of private property also implies caution about taxes above the minimum necessary for the rule of law and the common good. The freedom of contract must include the freedom not to contract.

It is sometimes said that no one dreams of capitalism—admittedly a narrow and problematic word. This must change. Rightly understood, capitalism is the economic component of the natural order of liberty. Capitalism offers wide ownership of property, fair and equal rules for all, strict adherence to the rules of ownership, opportunities for charity, and the wise use of resources. Everywhere it has really been tried, it has meant creativity, growth, abundance and, most of all, the economic application of the principle that every human being has dignity and should have that dignity respected.

And please don't tell me the free market is a myth simply because it has never existed in a pure form anywhere. Tell that to my grandfather. He came over to America with $35 in his pocket, yet almost all of his thirteen children went on to become middle class. Capitalism, rightly understood and pursued, has lifted untold millions out of abject poverty and allowed them to use skills and talents they would never have discovered, and to build opportunities their grandparents never dreamed were possible. The free economy is a dream worthy of our spiritual imaginations.

The good news is that the road to decline is not inevitable. Renewal is possible. A fatalist vision is not merely unsatisfying; it is unreal. We face a crisis that runs deep, but the outcome of the crisis is by no means determined. My message is not that of the placard-carrying street evangelist: "*The end is upon us.*" My message in the pages to follow is rather that the end of freedom and human flourishing in America is approaching... *unless*. In that word *unless* is hope—enough hope, I think, to inspire us and carry us to a new renaissance, a renewal of the moral foundation of the free economy.

In 1990 Kris Mauren and I created an institution dedicated to defending and promoting the free and virtuous society because we believed in that "unless." The Acton Institute for the Study of Religion and Liberty is committed to recovering certain perennial truths about political, economic, and religious freedom. Those perennial truths include some heady insights but also some down-to-earth, commonsense notions like not killing the goose that lays the golden egg; not binding down your most creative talent in a regulatory spider's web; and not teaching your citizens that they can all live at someone else's expense.

I have been saying these things long enough to know that some people will be delighted to "finally hear that from a preacher," while others will be shocked to hear it coming out of the mouth of a Catholic priest—and from a man who ran with Jane Fonda and Tom Hayden and the whole New Left Coast crowd of the early 1970s, no less. But they shouldn't be surprised. I grew up. And when I returned to my faith and went to seminary, I also recovered a deep understanding of the true end—the real purpose—of human freedom. In recovering that understanding I also rediscovered the wellspring of human liberty, and began to see the way forward.

But I'm running ahead of my story. It begins in homey surroundings, a pair of small facing apartments above the Lionel train store on Coney Island Avenue in Brooklyn, New York, where a five-year-old Italian kid was about to have an encounter with an elderly Jewish woman—a *refugee*, they called her—an encounter that would shape the course of his life, leaving him with an unquenchable desire to understand and promote human dignity.

CHAPTER 1

A Leftist Undone

I suppose the fact that I spent time on the left of the political spectrum isn't the surprising thing. I mean, I'm a New Yorker; I'm a child of the '60s; I went to seminary in the early 1980s, when a baptized form of Marxism was next to godliness. When you take all of that into account, my sojourn on the left has about it almost the inevitability of Marxist dialectic. What most people find surprising isn't that I was once a card-carrying lefty but that, despite my background, I somehow ended up as a passionate defender of the free economy, of liberty and limited government, of a traditional understanding of culture and morality, of all of those things that America's Founders held dear and that our country is now in danger of losing.

If I had to pick one memory from my childhood that might explain my passion for human freedom—both as a young man who believed that freedom was to be found in socialism, and later as a defender of limited government—it would be an experience from when I was a kid, one that remains imprinted indelibly on my memory more than half a century later.

She was a German immigrant. I was the grandson of Italian immigrants. I was about five. She was probably seventy-five. The setting of our little drama was a pair of facing apartments above the Lionel train store on Brooklyn's Coney Island Avenue—a neighborhood, I should add, miles from *the* Coney Island, the famed amusement park and beach that boasted then and still today the legendary wooden roller coaster, The Cyclone.

I say it wasn't *the* Coney Island, but all the same, what a place to grow up! All I had to do was walk out my front door and I was in the middle of a vibrant multi-ethnic experiment. Across the street was my Chinese friend, whose family, stereotypically enough, ran the neighborhood laundry. The luscious scent of starch mixed with steam greeted me when I would pop in to see if he could come out to play—his mother and grandmother ironing shirts to utter crispness as I waited for him.

If you turned left from our front door, you passed a hardware shop run by a thick-accented, tall, lanky Polish plumber and his family, who kept the pipes in that neighborhood flowing freely. If you turned right and walked to the corner of Coney Island and Avenue K, you came to a kosher pizza parlor. Where else besides Brooklyn or Tel Aviv would you find a kosher pizza parlor? It was all very exhilarating, and a little disorienting. For the longest time I didn't know the difference between Italians and Jews, other than that our kitchens smelled different.

Our closest neighbors were refugees, and when I say close, I mean very close.

Our apartment was one flight up from the street and it was a tiny one. The two front bedrooms overlooked the street with all its noise, bustle, and racket. One bedroom, where my two older brothers slept, was the size of a broom closet. My parents' bedroom had no door—the concept of privacy being, I have come to believe, a relatively recent invention, or at least one more thing that begins as a luxury but eventually graduates to become a "necessity of life" and thus a right. Instead of a door there was just an arch to separate the bedroom from the small living room decorated with floral-patterned wallpaper. Their bed was close to my crib—later a cot—which needed to be moved any time somebody wanted to get in the closet (one of two in the whole apartment). My sister, the eldest of the four children, slept on the couch in the living room.

This little apartment was mirrored by an identical apartment across an air shaft that also served as a roof access. One entered the apartment directly into the living room. A pivot to the left and there was the kitchen; a pivot to the right, and there was my parents' bedroom. Looking straight ahead, the window opened onto the air shaft and a roof level with our floor. There was, of course, no pastoral scene to be enjoyed, just the apartment across the way. If we wanted to borrow something from the neighbors, there was no picket fence to lean over—just slip out of our window and two steps would have you in front of theirs. And in that apartment, from which my mother would borrow milk or sugar from time to time, lived Mr. and Mrs. Schneider (I have altered some of the names in the biographical portions of this book for the privacy of those concerned).

I spoke to Mrs. Schneider on occasion, but I remember one particular day as if it were yesterday—I think because on that day one of those critical seeds was embedded deep into me. Much of what animates me now goes back to the encounter that bright spring day. I was at our kitchen window, peering into the Schneiders' kitchen window. Mrs. Schneider was standing there, wearing an apron. She was baking cookies—a particular and most delicious kind of Eastern European pastry known as rugelach. Today, you can buy a one-pound tin of rugelach online for $20 plus shipping, but back then there was just Mrs. Schneider, illuminated by the spring sun in a flowered dress and short sleeves rolling out the dough, putting in the walnuts doused in cinnamon and sugar, mixing all these together, rolling them up into tight crescents, placing them on a cookie sheet, and sliding them into her pale green Wedgewood oven. The process was rhythmic, almost hypnotic.

I was mesmerized by the sight, and soon enough a rich, intoxicating smell came wafting across to our kitchen. I couldn't have been more than five or six years old because my entire perspective of this memory was of leaning over a window sill that was relatively low to the ground. Mrs. Schneider had not once looked in my direction. She just kept putting one tray into the hot oven and pulling another tray out, in and out, rolling the dough in a rocking motion, until the moment the last tray was pulled. It was at that moment that Mrs. Schneider looked up, directly into my eyes, and with a slight smile said, "You'll come, I'll give you to eat," beckoning with her hand waving downward.

I scampered over the window sill and went over to her, holding up my greedy little hands, over which she placed a napkin and filled it with the rugelach—warm, flavorful, aromatic.

As she did so, I noticed that running up and down her forearm was a series of blue-tattooed numbers. I hadn't a clue what in the world that meant, but to be quite honest, I was more preoccupied with the goodies. And so I took my treasures and I went back into my kitchen. My mother came in and I told her that Mrs. Schneider had given me some treats. She seemed tired (and had a right to be: two jobs and no washing machine—which meant having to scrub the clothes on a wood and aluminum washboard in the bathtub). "That's great," she said. And I asked, "Mom... why, why does she have blue numbers on her arm?"

That was the day that I had my first lesson in moral philosophy.

We sat at the kitchen table, a white enameled piece with a red border chipped in places. Her weariness faded as she asked, "You know when you watch the cowboy shows, the Westerns?" "Yes," I replied. She said, "You know how the cowboys will lasso a calf and turn it upside down?" I said, "Yeah." She said, "What do they do then?" I said, "They put a brand on the back of the calf." She said, "Why do they do that?" And I said, "Because then everybody knows that that cow is owned by that cowboy."

She said, "That's right. Mr. and Mrs. Schneider came from a place where people treated them like animals. They thought they owned them. And what you saw on her arm was like a brand, and that's why you always have to be nice to Mr. and Mrs. Schneider because they saw their whole family killed. And they came here to our country for refuge. They're refugees and they came here to be safe."

That's when I first learned what the word "refugee" meant. I'd always thought the word just referred to another nationality. I would hear (and not always in politically correct language) that some Poles moved into the neighborhood, or that some Germans moved into the neighborhood, or that some French people moved into the neighborhood, or some refugees moved into the neighborhood. It was only now, sitting across the table from my mother, that I understood—refuge meant a place you come for safety.

My mother knew no formal philosophy, she never even graduated from high school; but there were some foundational truths she knew about anthropology and the intrinsic nature of human dignity, and she communicated to her five-year-old something perennially true: human beings must not be treated like animals. The worldview my mother was communicating to me was not about something people did (though there are plenty of things to be done) but about who people are, about something we possess in our very nature, by virtue of our mere existence, that says we cannot be treated as less than human. There is something unique, unrepeatable, and transcendent about human beings, and that something demands that their right to liberty be respected.

Left Turn

What I grasped less clearly, if at all, at the time was that this idea—this assumption so ingrained in the cultures and imagination of the West—was slipping out of our grasp, as the experience of Mrs. Schneider and her family showed. The slippage doesn't always begin with a group of opinion leaders sitting down to vote on a new anthropology—a novel understanding of man. And a new and debased anthropology doesn't always flare up into a world war or a holocaust. In the Germany of the '30s and '40s, the slippage in people's understanding of the dignity of man was seismic and cataclysmic. In the United States of recent years, it has been more subtle and gradual, a slow erosion of the foundation of our understanding of the human person.

An experience I had with a local parish priest when I was about ten or eleven years old comes to mind. I went to see him to ask some basic questions about our religion, questions that came to my mind as the result of a conversation I'd had with a non-Catholic classmate.

I can see now that the priest was about as disoriented as I was. This was in the midst of the Second Vatican Council; everything seemed up for grabs. The idea that religion should be, well, less religious (thanks in large part to Harvard theologian Harvey Cox's book, *The Secular City*), had already made the rounds in the parish rectory, so when that inquisitive pre-teen asked his priest how the Church could justify its position on—I don't even remember the question, but I do remember the answer—the priest just said, "Look, you don't want to be a religious fanatic. Instead of worrying about dogma, why don't you just read *Huckleberry Finn*?" That reply struck me—then, as it still does now—as shocking evidence of disregard for my search for spiritual meaning.

The young priest had directed me to Mark Twain. I went instead to the Brooklyn Yellow Pages and began calling and writing every Bible Chapel, spiritualist center, Kingdom Hall, and Christian Science Reading Room I could locate, asking for literature on their beliefs. Eventually I met some charismatics intent on witnessing their faith on the streets. They invited me to join a group of young people who walked the neighborhoods of New York vibrantly singing gospel songs. I experienced a sense of belonging with these folks, whose joy was palpable.

Had I stuck with them I might have made a career in gospel music because they would eventually become internationally known as the Brooklyn Tabernacle Choir. But I took another path. I left the Brooklyn of my childhood and moved to the West Coast where I continued my spiritual journey among what one might call experimental evangelicals—first in Seattle among the Jesus People.

But it wasn't long before I was less a wandering truth seeker than a prodigal son, a lost boy violating one taboo after another. The first—I stopped attending Mass. Within the next few years I would break many more. What I most needed, what would have most calmed the turbulence in the soul of that newly minted teenager, was not rebellion but reconciliation. But I didn't realize that at the time. Like so many people around me, I thought that breaking taboos was an emancipating experience, a necessary step on the path to self-discovery. I experienced liberty as license, thinking that the landscape could somehow be improved without a frame around it.

Unanchored from the traditions and friendships that had given my life some modicum of meaning and purpose, I found myself among new associates—comrades with whom I could speak freely about matters that until then I would have mentioned only in hushed tones in a dark confessional. These were the years of Woodstock and Stonewall, of the Beatles and Janis Joplin, a period that saw revolutions to overturn every standard in religion, the arts, fashion, architecture, literature, and sexuality. Sometimes it seemed like there was a new revolution every week. Everywhere I looked, some tradition was being bashed and the "new" and "relevant" uncritically embraced.

It was during this tumultuous period in my life, with the world so radically changing around me, that I turned to politics in an attempt to make sense of myself and my purpose on planet earth.

In those days, if there was a sit-in, I was sitting in it. If there was a demonstration, I was carrying a sign. I read Marx and found him boring. I listened to chic leftist intellectual Herbert Marcuse give a lecture and found it clear as linoleum. But the sense of change—that young people could do something that would count for the coming generations, that people could live free of the dominance of others—these were invigorating ideas.

I came to know Jane Fonda and her then husband Tom Hayden as I campaigned for Hayden in the 1976 California Democratic primary against incumbent U.S. Senator John Tunney. One particularly memorable interaction I had with Jane was at KPFK Radio in Los Angeles (the flagship station of the California left, the same place where the Symbionese Liberation Army had deposited its Patty Hearst tape) right around the time that Saigon tragically fell to the forces of North Vietnamese Communism. In the Hayden campaign I organized fundraisers and actively registered voters, and on one particular evening, I was standing with Jane in the rear parking lot of the Gay Community Services Center on Highland Boulevard after we had had a voters' registration drive there. As we were parting, I slipped a joint of marijuana into her hand. She was grateful.

"Thanks, Bob," (I was a Bob in those days) "Tom doesn't let me keep it in the house during the campaign."

"A fine feminist you are," I replied, as we hugged and parted.

After that our paths continued to cross from time to time as I became active in a panoply of radical causes that Fonda and Hayden also supported: I campaigned for women's rights, for gay rights, for the farm workers' boycott of Gallo wine—I could go on and on.

It's not an exaggeration to say that I had the feeling I was deep inside a revolution. When my old comrades from those days hear about me now, the eyebrows go up. When I tell them that not only did I find my way out of the "New Left" of '70s L.A., but that in learning to love liberty and limited government I also found my way back to my Christian faith—well, for my old friends on the left, it's just too much. When they discover that this post-Vatican II Catholic priest is the president of an international think tank dedicated to promoting a society rooted in unchanging moral truths about good and evil, to championing the free economy, private property, and the rule of law as the great safeguards of the poor—well, if they're still like my old activist friends from my days in L.A., they shake their heads in bewilderment.

What was the moment that I began my journey away from the left?

One hot summer afternoon a little band of my friends and I spent a good part of the day in several different protest demonstrations before we ended up back at my Hollywood apartment. Sitting around the living room, we recounted the events of the day and—idealistic as we were—expressed our dreams about what the world would look like "when the revolution comes." Everyone would be equal. There would be no more classism, homophobia, and sexism. And it was in that relaxed and trusting atmosphere that I said something to the effect that "Yes, and when the revolution comes we'll all be able to shop at Gucci."

There was silence. The smoke stood still in the air. (I prefer not to say what kind of smoke it was.)

My good friend Ann (I used to call her my Lesbyterian Trotskyite) was sitting on the floor next to me. She leaned over and put her head on my shoulder.

"Gucci?"

"Yes," I replied. "It's a metaphor for the kind of society we are seeking to build, where everyone will have access to quality goods and services."

"Gucci?" she asked again, looking around the room at the other comrades. "I don't think you're really a socialist."

She seemed to know before I did.

Not long after that I made the mistake that would prove fatal to my leftist ideology. I didn't realize it, but it began when I visited the apartment of an activist friend of mine, who introduced me to a new resident of his apartment complex. They walked me to my car, which was coincidentally parked directly behind the car of the new neighbor. I immediately noticed some bumper stickers on his car that were very politically incorrect (we used the phrase unironically in those days). An argument ensued, wherein I pontificated about the need for the redistribution of wealth, or some such thing. The fierce debate only subsided when the neighbor fixed me with a stare and observed, "You are delightfully dumb, Sirico. I am going to undertake the task of educating you."

To engage an intelligent and informed conservative in a conversation stretching over not an elevator ride or a meal but many weeks and months was a new and eye-opening experience. My newfound friend supplied me with a little library of liberty. (Some of those titles are listed at the end of each chapter.) Gradually, over the next six months, the ideas from those texts caused something inside me to shift. They set off an intellectual avalanche. Slowly at first but then more and more rapidly, a voracious hunger to learn more—not merely about economics and politics, but about the fundamental truths of human existence—overwhelmed my shallow leftism.

I had long been interested in exploring deep questions, but I had gone about it in a haphazard fashion. Now I began to approach these matters in a logical sequence as one question led to another, and then to another and another. A comprehensive, coherent, and integrated vision began to emerge, like a picture from scattered puzzle pieces on a table.

The first things I read at my new friend's behest were on the question of rights. I had spoken passionately for the rights of various minorities, but gradually I came to understand the real meaning of "rights" for the first time. I began to see that it makes no sense to speak of collective rights if one does not understand what the rights of the human person are first. If, for instance, women or farm workers or gays have any rights, it must be because they possess human rights—not female or farm worker or gay rights. Eventually I came to look at the idea of rights from the perspective of the Declaration of Independence—to see that rights are not granted by the State, but that we possess them by the very fact of our existence, and that they are based on our nature, not our social circumstance, class or group affiliation. Such rights are "unalienable," because while governments can protect, or obfuscate, or even violate these rights, they are nonetheless inherent in the person by nature. Our rights predate the human institution of government and cannot *justly* be taken away by institutions or other human beings.

From the basic concept of rights I went on to property rights—an idea that initially struck me as utter heresy. How can one speak of mere material property as having rights, over against the needs of human beings? Finally, through readings and my running debate with my new friend, I realized that property rights *are* human rights. Putting it simply, if a human being has no right to some things he owns—for example, the land he owns and farms to feed his family—he has no means by which he can provide for himself and hence no meaningful right to live. I was blown over. How could I have missed something so obvious?

I kept reading about economics—supply and demand, the division of labor, economies of scale, and competition. They were all topics I'd heard of before, even phrases I had used. But now I began to understand the concepts for the first time. I gradually realized that these ideas were not an invention by biased intellectuals but rather descriptive terms for features of the world that are intrinsic to human reality itself. Little by little the logic of what I was reading ate away at my leftist assumption that economics was about money and property and production—and not human beings. The kind of economics I was learning—mostly from economists of the "Austrian school," men such as Ludwig von Mises and Friedrich Hayek—was not an abstract academic discipline that numbed the minds of students with logarithms and equations spewed across the blackboard in the university classroom. It dealt with *human choice and action* more than mathematics. Along the way I came to understand the utilitarian case for the free market, for human liberty rightly understood, for the necessity of free choice, and for private property. I came to see, for instance, that prices in a free market contain a wealth of information that no centralized planner could possibly possess, and therefore they better promote economic prosperity—which means that millions of real live people on the margins live longer, healthier, and happier lives.

I came to see that competition, as long as it is guided by the rule of law, is a method for improving the quality and price of goods and services. Producers were competing with each other, yes, but it was a competition in serving others in an ever more excellent way. This was not a "dog eat dog" situation but rather a system that incentivized service to others. Competition "plans" the economy for people in a way that is far superior to any centralized "economic planning" dreamt up on the left. The most productive thing the government can do for the economy is not "planning." It's enforcement of the rule of law so that there's a level playing field, and more goods and services are produced.

I further came to realize that competition is only one of many features of the market economy. Another is cooperation, in free association. When we shop, when we invest, when we sell or buy anything, we have to seek the consent of another. This benefits both parties. Workers cooperate in the workforce, too. And employees cooperate with employers in a mutually dependent relationship. This is not exploitation. It is peaceful cooperation, and it plays as strong a role in the forward motion of markets as does the competitive spirit.

Finally, it is not all about dollars and cents. Philanthropy, charity, voluntarism, activism, and care for family and the poor are all related to the same impulses that drive the market economy: the peaceful and free association of people in the service of others.

But I soon realized that all of this raised even more basic questions. I needed to revisit the question of rights. I was coming to understand more fully the connection between freedom on the one hand and human dignity, human creativity, and human flourishing on the other. A right use of freedom has tended to encourage human dignity, creativity, and flourishing. But why should we care about those things? Why value human creativity? Why even believe that human beings possess dignity and rights? The economic system I was coming to embrace assumed rather than defended the value of all these things—something very easy to miss, since most of us share these sentiments. But I wanted more than sentiments, more than appeals to consensus opinion. I had been there and done that. As I knew all too well, sentiments come and go. The consensus of today may be the unspeakable in the totalitarian regime of tomorrow.

I wanted to know why. And for this I would have to go deeper than "*homo economicus*," the imaginary perfectly self-interested human being—a concept that is sometimes useful for economic analysis but an inadequate representation of the full range of human motivations and capacities, *of human beings as we really are.*

Suddenly, it was as though the lights went on in a room, and I could make out the various objects that I had been stumbling over for the previous decade. The questions I had long let go begging became urgent—and I began to see that the answers were within my grasp. As I reached firmer ground than mere personal preference and gut feeling, I realized that the questions I was asking of Friedrich Hayek and Milton Friedman were questions I had heard before. They were more profound formulations of the simple queries that the tall nun had posed to our First Holy Communion Class when I was a child.

Sister would stand in the midst of sixty hushed Brooklyn seven-year-olds, there in the basement at St. Rose of Lima parish, and hold aloft the Baltimore Catechism. She would ask question after question, and we would read the response:

"Children, Who made the world?"

"God made the world," we would respond in unison.

"Who is God?"

"God is the Supreme Being, infinite, Creator of heaven and earth, and of all things."

"What is man?"

"Man is a creature composed of body and soul, and made to the image and likeness of God"

"Why did God make you?"

"God made me to know Him, to love Him and to serve Him in this world, and to be happy with Him forever in the next."

What that nun, who was probably little more than a teenager herself and almost certainly had no degree in philosophy or theology, instilled in me is this: The world that surrounds me is understandable. Our minds are reliable tools for knowing that world, which is itself permeated with meaning. My life, too, has meaning and therefore dignity because I have an intentional origin and an intentional destiny that begins with the goodness of this world and yet transcends anything I can see with my eyes or touch with my hands.

We are, moreover, made in the image of a Creator to be creative (like him). The God we see operative in the first pages of the Bible is not a passive entity. He engages, indeed, engenders the world. And at the summit of this creation are the beings created in his very likeness and image: the human family. It should come as no surprise, then, that the first words spoken to man and woman constitute a calling to a similar creativity: "Be fruitful and multiply, and fill the earth."

Had Sister said all this to us at the time, I would not have understood. Even into the years that were still to come—as I grew to understand economic realities in light of the truth about God and human beings—I was like a man groping my way blindfolded through a wardrobe full of new treasures. I didn't have the categories or the tools to make sense of things. Mystery, I read once, is not *not* knowing. It is knowing so much that you find yourself unable to express it all. And yet that Sister laid a foundation that sustained me through all the questions and eventually allowed me to reach a place where I finally could speak the words of St. Augustine from my own heart: *Sero te amavi, pulchritudo tam antiqua et tam nova, sero te amavi—Late have I loved you, O Beauty so ancient and so new, late have I loved you!* Over a period of several months I came once again to know that there was a God, and that he was personal. I knew that the world was formed at his design and infused with his purpose, and that he fashioned the human race in his likeness, etching into us his own nature. And I knew that he wanted to be known by this world, and that he had revealed himself in the person of his Son, Jesus Christ, who had established a Church on the earth to carry forth this message.

I want to be clear about this journey of mine to faith and freedom—about how they are and are not related. It wasn't that the Catholic Church I had grown up in had officially endorsed the prudential judgments of the free market thinkers I had come to embrace. The Catholic Church does not—and never has—"taught economics." Rather, its focus is on the principles that ought to inform how we think about and act in economic life. But the Catholic faith, as I began to dust it off and rediscover it, did provide solid reasons for valuing many of the things these free market thinkers sought to sustain and encourage. The process of spiritual renewal was not instantaneous. In fact, I am still in the midst of it almost forty years later. But there was a day in my late twenties when—surrounded by an unlikely set of intellectual companions, most of them either nonreligious or, in the case of Ayn Rand, positively anti-religious—I knew that the prodigal son had begun his long walk back home.

And it is from within the harbor of that home that I can see things that were once obscure to me. My radical friends and I back in 1970s California spoke often of justice. But surely it is not merely justice that any of us seek in society, or in our lives. Justice—treating people as they deserve to be treated—is a fundamental civil and moral requirement. But by itself it is a rather meager necessity. What we really want is a society that is just, yes, but also one that is suffused with charity and mercy—virtues that no legislature can produce or enact, virtues that can raise up armies of men and women who are prepared to go out and tend the vulnerable at great personal sacrifice.

After all, at the Last Judgment, when each of us will stand before God, I doubt any of us is going to be demanding justice. I, for one, will plead for mercy.

If justice and mercy are to thrive in our society, I understand now, we need to protect the institutions of liberty, "the delicate fruit of a mature civilization,"[1] as the Victorian statesman and historian Lord Acton called it. We must work strenuously to safeguard the liberty that our security and prosperity depend on.

Our civilization is, I believe, deeply vulnerable. What happens when we have our prosperity but lose our meaning? What happens when we lose a sense of ourselves as transcendent beings? What happens when we are no longer able or inclined to defend the institutions and ideas that have enabled our prosperity and still guarantee our freedom?

That belief, in the dangers to our liberty—to our dignity and capacity for flourishing, to our identity as a people dedicated to freedom and justice—that realization, is the animating force behind this book.

The good news (and the other reason I am writing this book) is that Karl Marx was wrong. Civilizations are not directed by any fatalistic process of dialectical materialism. God is in his heaven and free men still walk upon the earth. Class envy and class warfare can, have, and will again give way to class encounter and cooperative creativity within a competitive marketplace.

During World War II, economist Friedrich Hayek warned about "the road to serfdom," a road marked by increasing government control of the economy. The United States has been on that road for many years now. But there is another road, a road to freedom, a road that we can reach and walk if we marshal the old virtues of fortitude and thrift and courage to make the journey. The chapters that follow will continue to limn the contours of such a journey, both its pitfalls and its promise.

Suggestions for Further Reading

F. A. Hayek, *The Road to Serfdom*, 50th anniversary ed. (University of Chicago, 1994).

Paul Heyne, *The Economic Way of Thinking* (Prentice Hall, 2005).

Instruction on Certain Aspects of the "Theology of Liberation" (Congregation for the Doctrine of the Faith, 1984), available at www.vaticanva/roman_curia/congregations/cfaith/documents/rc_con_cfaith_doc_19840806_theology-liberation_en.html.

Thomas Sowell, *Basic Economics: A Common Sense Guide to the Economy* (Basic Books, 2007).

CHAPTER 2

Why You Can't Have Freedom without a Free Economy

Q: How can you defend the "right" to private property? Only people have rights—not things! The supposed right to private property just protects the power of the rich to oppress the poor. Doesn't the earth belong to everyone?

■ ■ ■

A: Property rights are personal rights. "Property" is not some thing out there in the world. It's a relationship between a thing or an idea and a human being. If men and women aren't secure in the right to property—not just to consume things, but to create with them and even to accumulate them—then they're not secure in their human rights. Other human rights (to freedom of speech and of worship, for example) tend to be eroded wherever property rights are violated. Without property rights people are not secure in their basic livelihood, either. Every scheme of redistribution that has defied the right to private property has created more poverty. The right to private property is not absolute, but it is a basic human right. When and where that right is respected, people and whole societies flourish.

■ ■ ■

A lot of my old friends from the 1970s ardently defend what they call personal freedom while happily supporting policies that shrink our economic freedom. They have missed a lesson of history that eluded me for a long time as well: lose your economic freedom, and soon enough you will lose your other freedoms as well. Friedrich Hayek, an Austrian economist who would go on to win the Nobel Prize, described the process in a book he wrote during World War II. As Hayek explained, people don't intend to trade away their most basic freedoms. They just want more economic equality and more financial security. But the result is always the same, as Hayek made clear in the title of his book—*The Road to Serfdom*. Unless the relationship between "personal" and "economic" freedom is really understood, both can easily be lost.

Sometimes even people who speak the same language do not understand one another. My undergraduate studies were enriched by a year I spent living and studying in England. It was particularly educational—sometimes funny, sometimes confusing, and sometimes embarrassing—to discover linguistic differences between British and American idioms.

Soon after I moved into my hostel, some of the other blokes (guys) on the same floor invited the Yanks (Americans) out to visit a local pub (bar). We accepted and pretty soon found ourselves sitting in the midst of a bunch of British and American guys getting to know one another and asking questions about what things were like in each others' country. The waitress soon came by to take our orders, and as she went around the semi-circle I noticed that she was not writing down any of our diverse drink orders. She returned shortly with all of our pints and half-pints: Guinness and Harp; hard cider; pale or amber lager; pale or amber ale. These were all balanced on a large and heavy tray which she handled with admirable precision.

Her professionalism in remembering all the orders, placing each with the fellow who had ordered it, and not spilling a drop seemed to me a feat of expert competency, so I decided to commend her by saying, "Miss, you are a real pro!"

A solemn and embarrassed silence descended over our group. People from other tables who had heard my "compliment" stared at me. I had the sense of having committed a great social blunder, but I had no clue what it was. I turned to a fellow sitting next to me and asked what happened. In a high British accent he replied, "You have just called the young lady a prostitute," he said, and left me to wallow in my agony.

As George Bernard Shaw observed, America and England are "two nations separated by a common language."

But the story illustrates a more generally applicable point: it's important to define your terms and to understand what you are really talking about. That goes for politics as much as it does for prostitution (and not just because some politicians may behave like prostitutes). Freedom is an idea at the heart of the American Experiment. But what exactly is freedom, rightly understood?

Freedom and Chaos

Freedom is a word that can mean dramatically different things to different people in different settings. The kind of freedom that leads to human flourishing—and that is sustainable over time—is freedom in a much richer sense than what many people mean by freedom today.

Let me take the point even further. True freedom is actually the opposite of what has been called "freedom" at some times and some places. One example from the previous century illustrates what I mean.

The Constitution guaranteed freedom of speech, freedom of assembly, and freedom of religion. I'm not talking about the U.S. Constitution, although the same could be said of it. I'm talking about the Soviet Constitution of 1924. And after that constitution took effect, political dissidents were brutally suppressed; priests, ministers, and rabbis were deported to the Gulag; houses of worship were shuttered; and the press was hammered into line with an iron fist. Lenin, Stalin, Khrushchev, and Brezhnev did all of this even while the text of the nation's constitution proclaimed a paradise of liberty. In the minds of those men, freedom wasn't about the God-given rights of individuals that must be respected by governments. It was about free scope for the will of the proletariat—for whom they were the only legitimate representatives, of course.

This kind of confusion about freedom didn't end with the fall of the Berlin Wall in 1989. Visit almost any major university in America and you'll find individuals praising freedom while admiring ruthless totalitarians, usually without the least sense of irony or awareness of the contradiction. And often the totalitarians being praised are the ones who, while busily stamping out freedom, are reassuring everyone that they're stamping in order to free the people, stamping in pursuit of "national liberty and equality," stamping for "the pacific co-existence and fraternal collaboration of peoples."[1]

Why does all of this matter? When liberty and freedom can mean so many different things—sometimes diametrically opposing things—we are no longer free to have a meaningful conversation about political freedom, at least not until we talk about what exactly we mean when we use these terms.

To some, freedom means nothing more than the license to do whatever they want, when they want—as when a wild teenager longs to be "free of all these stupid rules." To others, freedom means the liberty to worship God freely according to the dictates of their conscience, or the right to govern themselves through duly elected representatives. President Franklin Roosevelt talked about freedom in terms of government-supplied security and even welfare—freedom from want, freedom from fear, and so forth. But the Founders who wrote the U.S. Constitution thought about liberty as limiting what government was allowed to do, and their understanding of freedom was tied up in the old notion of freedom in Christ, which is why they repeatedly emphasized that the constitutional republic they had formed was, as John Adams put it, "made only for a moral and religious people" and "wholly inadequate to the government of any other."[2]

Freedom has a wide variety of meanings—some people think of it as the ability to do what they know they ought to do, even when it is not attractive at the moment, as when a lonely husband remains faithful to his wife while on a business trip, or a recovered alcoholic has achieved enough self-control to live a life of sobriety. For still others, it means what the great twentieth century Dominican theologian Servais Pinckaers called "freedom for excellence," as when a pianist strives to master a demanding piece by Rachmaninoff and is finally able to play it with ease and fluidity.

So let's look at what freedom is and can be. This need not be a terribly abstract and philosophical examination. We can use our common sense and elementary logic. The best of philosophy is looking simply but seriously at things as they really are. Let's begin with what we know, each of us, about ourselves.

I think it can be easily observed that there is something innate in the human heart that responds positively to the idea of liberty—no doubt in more than one sense of the word. People have pledged their lives, their fortunes, and their sacred honor to its defense. Over the course of the last century, countless men and women risked their lives to flee from totalitarian domination into a realm of freedom. People—perhaps even some we have known personally—swam shark-infested waters, climbed electrified fences, catapulted over barriers, dug their way through tunnels, and outran guard dogs and border guards—all to escape bondage and reach a place where they could breathe free. To be aware of what human beings have sacrificed for freedom is to understand that freedom is not a garnish on life but one of the central quests of the human experience. The human heart has a natural orientation toward liberty. We are built this way, regardless of our religion or ethnicity; indeed, all men are endowed with liberty and a deep desire for it.

What is it about freedom that makes it so irresistible a goal—and yet still so complex an idea that we can become confused about what it is? Alexis de Tocqueville—perhaps the greatest observer of the uniqueness of America—can help us get a grasp on it. "Freedom is, in truth, a sacred thing," he insists. "There is only one thing else that better deserves the name: that is virtue." And then he asks, "What is virtue if not the free choice of what is good?"[3]

The yearning for freedom is built into our bones. Of course, human beings are corporeal like other animals. We are bodies, subject to the laws of physics, chemistry, and biology. But unlike other animals, the human person has the additional capacity to transcend himself. Even non-believers can observe this aspect of human personhood, for example when a person falls in love and discovers more of himself or herself, even while giving that self away to the other. We also experience this transcendent aspect of the human person in the exaltation we feel in beautiful music, great art, or poetry.

From Reason to the Reason for Property

Both animals and human beings have bodies, but animals are bound to things by their instincts, whereas we humans relate to things by our minds. Our reason means that we can reflect upon ourselves and what we are doing. We can actually think about our thoughts! We think and are dependent on the use of reason.[4] The mind is what makes human beings distinctly human. Consider the fact that the human mammal is one of the most vulnerable of all animals: we have no prehensile tail that enables us to swing away from danger, no wings with which we can take flight from the predator, no fangs or fierce claws or thick hide to ward off our enemies. The human person lives by reason, apprehending reality and ordering reality, integrating, understanding, remembering, and building.

It is this rational relationship we human beings have to nature that gives rise to property. Property, you see, is not this or that physical object. Property is a relationship between a person and a thing or idea. To own property is to be in a particular kind of relationship with something in the world—a relationship, moreover, that is recognized by others in the community. Some animals have a recognizable if rudimentary sense of what we might call ownership, of course—as when one beaver knows that another beaver possesses a particular dam. But what is most illuminating in such comparisons are the differences. A beaver cannot sell his dam or buy one from another beaver, he cannot lease the dam, and he does not use his dam for collateral to borrow money to launch a business. But human property owners are able to do all these things with the property they own—because property exists in the context of shared human reason.

Why is private property essential? Why shouldn't all property be owned by all? The scarcity of physical things is a feature of the world that we cannot escape. This fact of scarcity means that there is a potential conflict over who is going to use things and how. We can struggle with each other to grab and keep what we can for ourselves. Or we can use a system rooted in private ownership, which permits us to trade, give gifts, or share based on our own free will. This is the peaceful solution to the problem of scarcity.

It also so happens that private property demonstrates the interpenetration between our physical bodies and our capacity for transcendence. We engage nature with labor that our reason plans and directs—and produce something that did not previously exist. Not just another beaver dam exactly the same as the ones beavers have been building for millennia, but a Chartres Cathedral, a *Mona Lisa*—or an electric light bulb, a smallpox vaccine, a revolution in agriculture that lifts millions of people out of dire poverty or, more modestly, a garden or orchard that feeds a family and expresses a particular gardener's thoughtful stewardship of the land.

These things are possible because we don't just relate to the material world in an immediate or temporary manner. The relationship of human beings to things is not merely a relationship of consumption. It is also one of reason and creativity—and it is that relationship that makes the institution of private property possible. "The right to private property" is not merely control over a physical object, as my dog Theophilus might possess a bone. Rather the right to property is wrapped up in a person's capacity to apply his intellect to matter and ideas, to look ahead, to plan and steward the use of that possession. Just as other fundamental human rights are not created by the state but are possessed by virtue of a person's existence and nature, so also the right to private property is *recognized* rather than *granted* by the government.

This right to private property is not absolute—no one, no matter how rich, has the right to buy up the whole surface of the earth, or even to deny bread he owns to a starving neighbor who has absolutely no recourse for survival[5]—but it is sacred because it has such a close connection to human beings as creatures made in the image of God, creatures placed in the context of scarcity and given a capacity to reason, create, and transcend. The best thing that politicians can do in regard to property is to enact and enforce just laws in accordance with natural law—to protect people from having their belongings unjustly confiscated.

This is why cultures that have systematically attacked and undermined the right to private property have tended to wither, and those civilizations that have managed to extend the right to private property to an ever greater number of their people have tended to thrive. Here I can't help but think of an Acton Institute interview of the historian and sociologist Rodney Stark. He was discussing why China, which a thousand years ago was ahead of the West in many ways, fell behind technologically and eventually in measures of societal well-being, such as life expectancy among the poor. The story is immensely complicated, but it boils down to one issue—private property:

> One of the great sad stories is that something that looked like the start of a real, honest, industrial revolution started in China about the tenth century. They had some small iron smelters and they started getting bigger and bigger and bigger, and people who owned them kept reinvesting and increased production and they got bigger and bigger. And eventually, the Mandarins discovered this was going on and that ordinary people were getting rich. They stopped it. They closed it down. The whole thing stopped and went away. Look, a great historian of Asia put it well. He said, private property is not secure and that's the first, and last, and total answer to why there was no development in the East.[6]

The positive side of this coin is that a thousand years later many Asian countries have begun to thrive economically as they have moved away from command-and-control economies and begun extending economic freedom to larger and larger numbers of their people—imperfectly as in any human society, but still in a dramatic shift toward expanded property rights and economic liberty.

That property rights are related to the well-being of men and women shouldn't surprise us. As we've seen, they are an outgrowth of human intelligence and transcendence. Property comes into existence in this interplay and overlap of human physicality and spirituality. Thus throughout history it has proven difficult to safeguard personal freedoms like the freedom of speech in the absence of property rights. If you are to have the right to free speech, but are not permitted to publish a book at a private publisher, or to own a newspaper or TV or radio station, or (increasingly) even to post an opinion online because the government has begun to treat the internet as if it owns it, then in what practical sense can you be said to have the right to free speech?

The same is true of religion. If the state strips away our economic freedom to decide how and where we use our private means to compensate doctors, nurses, and physical therapists in exchange for medical care, if the government comes to control all of this as if these medical skills and private exchanges were somehow the government's property, then it suddenly becomes easier for the government to infringe upon one's right to religious freedom in certain important ways. Consider the mandate issued by the Obama administration's Department of Health and Human Services in early 2012, requiring religious institutions to provide abortifacient drugs, sterilization, and contraception coverage as part of their health insurance programs even if those religious groups are morally opposed to doing so. The fact that a seventh of the nation's economy had already been placed under the control of the federal government by Obamacare—the fact that so many in our culture were comfortable with such a massive government intervention in the private sector—made it much easier for HHS to issue such a mandate.

It is very instructive to review the progress of the passage of Obamacare. It was initially supported by the American Bishops' conference, but eventually lost their support out of fear that it lacked a sufficient "conscience clause" exempting Church institutions from covering services deemed immoral by the Church.

Independence of conscience is not so easy to maintain when you aren't independent of government purse strings. When a religious institution becomes dependent on the state, political control eventually follows, as surely as night follows day. The old adage, "He who drinks the king's wine sings the king's songs," seems applicable here.

The king in this case, the Obama administration, has brought other weapons to bear in its ongoing attack on religious freedom. One is the power of the president's bully pulpit. In a subtle but powerful rhetorical shift, administration figures have begun speaking of the "freedom of worship" rather than the "freedom of religion."[7] While the two phrases sound similar, the difference between them raises certain questions: Does the freedom to worship include a social dimension? May one, for example, worship with others? If so, where? May a group assemble and purchase property for this purpose? What if their religion admonishes them to teach children, or tend to the sick? May they build schools, hospitals, and universities? You see the problem? With only "freedom of worship," religion all too easily becomes something quarantined from the public square, something done in private and only in private, if you have any sense of secular decorum.

Personal liberty is interconnected with economic liberty. It is dangerous to surrender one's economic independence by accepting subsidies, even with the intention of accomplishing good. Government largesse is all too likely at some point to carry with it requirements at odds with one's deepest principles and morals.

The debate over the Obama administration's contraception mandate was not fundamentally about contraception or even cooperation with abortion. It is fundamentally about religious freedom—and about the meaning of private institutions in society: Should we look to the government to provide everything that a society needs—almost as though the government had resources outside of society? Is there a role for a truly private sector in charitable works, in economic decision-making, in education and the moral formation of society—a role apart from the work of government? Ought we to maintain, in any real and effective way, a distinction between society and the state? Or is every obligation of society to be subsumed, subsidized, regulated, and implemented by the state? Not many would welcome such a state of affairs, and yet such has been the trajectory of the American government for many years now.

Property in Practice

The earth is God's first gift for the sustenance of human life, and it is given to all for their use. But what does that mean in practice? That anyone can have anything at any time? The earth does not yield its fruits without a human response to God's gift. Human labor and creativity are intimately associated with human ownership and stewardship of God's creation.

Many societies—and the Christian Church—have experimented with the idea of communal ownership, and have discovered that there is a significant difference between ownership by the state and ownership by a religious community. All property must be owned by someone. So when we speak of collective ownership we are usually talking about ownership by the state. And concentrated government ownership of property is a recipe for disaster. This is no longer a matter of theoretical conjecture. A political party and half a continent ran the experiment beginning in the nineteenth century. "Property is theft!" cried Pierre-Joseph Proudhon—a conviction which inspired the first meeting in 1868 of what eventually became the Communist International. Twenty years earlier, Karl Marx summed up socialist theory in the single phrase: "abolition of private property." The doctrine begot a full-blown political movement by the turn of the century, and became the foundational teaching of many of the most brutal regimes in the twentieth century.

The central delusion of all forms of socialism was the belief that an economy can be based on collective ownership. But collective ownership turns out to be no ownership at all, or else—and this is what inevitably happens, in practice—ownership by the privileged political class, that is, people with the most power. Without private property, the state pretends to rule on everyone's behalf, replacing exploitation of private citizen by private citizen with the much more horrible exploitation of the whole society by a revolutionary political elite. Perhaps nothing in history has wrought suffering on a wider scale than this doctrine.

Not only would-be tyrants and socialists have decried property ownership. The Pilgrims, good and godly men, were victims of the collective property delusion. In 1620, the Plymouth Colony held pastures and produce in common as a matter of law, out of a mistaken sense that shared property would be more efficiently productive. The result was economic chaos, disease, starvation, death, and the near extinction of the first New England settlers.

William Bradford, governor of the colony, said the collective property policy "was found to breed much confusion and discontent and retard much employment that would have been to their benefit and comfort."[8]

So he drew clear lines of ownership. The result was the first plentiful harvest and the first bountiful Thanksgiving. Even today we give thanks to God who commanded us to till and keep the land and forbade us from taking what belongs to others.

Privately held property (which can also be communal, as in families and monasteries), tends to diffuse power and influence throughout society. Private property confers on individuals and families an area of autonomy that is necessary for human freedom and civil liberties. Property is the ordinary means by which the human family carries out the commandment to have dominion over the earth. When property is in private hands, it must be cared for and used to serve others if the owners hope to gain from that property. Where property rights are respected and a free market exists, productive resources will tend to flow in the direction of people who can care for them best and best use them to serve others. For example, if Family A makes terrible use of a peach orchard, failing to prune, fertilize, and water it, or to harvest the peaches in a timely manner, their orchard business will eventually go broke, and they will sell it to someone else. If the land is best suited for an orchard, it's likely to eventually end up in the hands of Family B, competent orchardists who can make a go of the orchard and run it as a sustainable enterprise—supplying their fellow man with delicious and healthful fruit.

The free enterprise system isn't perfect, of course, for the simple reason that human beings are not perfect. Every vice you see among human beings, you will also see in the markets they create. But markets are far superior to the alternative. Publicly owned property easily falls into disrepair because no one in particular has the incentive to maintain it. Hence the institution of property provides a foundation for the exercise of stewardship responsibilities—caring for what belongs to you. After all, if goods are marketable, they have value not only to their owner but to potential future owners as well. For that reason there is a strong incentive not to over-utilize or otherwise harm the resource, an incentive that is missing when the person using the property lacks a sense of ownership over it.

Now some people actually think that the Bible somehow condemns the idea of private property. Referring to Acts 2:44 and to a story in Acts 5 in the New Testament, various strains of theological commentators have expounded on the early practice of the Christian community to share with one another ("they had all things common"), and the monastic ideal it later inspired. It is untrue, however, that private property was either abolished or prohibited in the early Church. The case of Ananias and Sapphira (in Acts 5) clearly shows this. The couple decided to sell some land that they owned, but rather than turn all the money over to the apostles, they held back a portion and lied about it to Peter. Note what Peter says in response to the deception: "While it remained unsold, did it not remain your own? And after it was sold, was it not at your disposal?... You have not lied to men but to God." The moral problem here was obviously not the ownership of private property—which is clearly affirmed—but the deception the couple engaged in.

Christian sharing is not the same thing as socialism, for a very simple reason. Christian charity consists of free-will offerings motivated by love; socialist redistribution is brought about only by force. That the experiment in Acts 2 did not become the doctrine of the church is seen by the fact that the apostle Paul never mandates it for his churches, but rather depends upon their voluntary charity to support missionary projects.

In any case, it would be difficult to make sense of the commandment in Exodus Chapter 20—"Thou shalt not steal"—if the Bible were not presupposing the validity of private property. You cannot steal something, after all, if no one owns it.

These examples only scratch the surface of the biblical case for private property. The evidence in favor of private property is neither subtle nor easy to miss in the Bible. Nor is it easy to miss in the sacred texts of other major religions. The moral injunction against theft—common to most all religions—implies a moral injunction against violating the established boundaries of property ownership (which admittedly may differ from culture to culture), and logically confirms the moral legitimacy of property ownership to begin with.

Injunctions against theft protect not just individuals but also the common good (which is the sum total of what people need as individuals and as groups). Cultures rife with theft simply cannot create new wealth over the long haul, since those who are chronically robbed lose the incentive to work and create new wealth, while those who do the robbing find it easier to steal than to earn. Soon cultures of sloth and expropriation develop. More than this, some of the bitterest and bloodiest struggles in world history have come about because of failures to respect the biblical commandment against theft.

Trade, Contracts, and Interest Rates

The opposite of a culture of theft and moral chaos is a market governed by the rule of law, one in which contracts are enforced, the politically unconnected are allowed to trade in the market just as freely as the politically well-connected are, and entrepreneurs and investors are able to agree freely on mutually satisfying terms, based on a transparent system of interest rates. Trade, contracts, and interest rates may seem to be mundane subjects, but these institutions are fundamental aspects of economic liberty—and concrete guarantors of freedom more generally.

Let's take a brief look at each of the three.

The freedom to trade is a necessary adjunct to private property rights. A secure right to property means little if people are not permitted to exchange their property for other property that they desire more. This is the essence of trade. International trade organizations, protracted debates about globalization, and convoluted trade agreements have turned the field of international trade into a complex matter, but trade is, at its root, simply an exchange between two parties who both stand to benefit.

Like a shepherd bartering with a blacksmith in times gone by, trading wool for iron tools, modern people trade goods and services internationally because the other party has something they need or want and they are willing to give up something they have in return. Tariffs, subsidies, embargoes, and other government distortions of free trade are justified on the basis of the benefit they provide to some domestic industry or other—but they do enormous damage by way of higher prices for everyone, and foreclosed opportunities for struggling entrepreneurs in developing countries are less widely publicized.

If all people always kept their promises to each other, and also had perfect communication skills, trade could take place without the need for written agreements. But because the economic world is populated by fallible people, the institution of the contract arose to provide security against broken promises and miscommunications. Contracts ensure the title to property and the freedom to exchange that property; they fulfill our desire to be able to make agreements to exchange property that are binding over time.

A stable, consistent regime of contract law permits people to plan for the future, and rewards those who keep their commitments, thus assisting people in trusting and getting along with other people, even people very different from themselves—and even people they don't know.

Contracts reward those who associate in peace, while at the same time providing negative sanctions for those who do not keep their commitments. Over time, the institution of binding agreements dramatically enhances productive cooperation among far-flung individuals. New possibilities for creating wealth are unleashed when people know they can rely on the agreements they make with people they have never even met—perhaps people on the other side of the world.

Okay, you have waded with me through a brief discussion of the importance of contracts and free trade. Let me explain just one more technical feature of a free economy, and we will move on to more colorful material.

Since at least the era of the Hebrew Scriptures, the interpretation of key biblical texts that seem to unilaterally condemn payment and receipt of interest (Exodus 22:25, Leviticus 25:35–37, Deuteronomy 23:19–20, and Psalms 15:5) has placed the entire practice under a moral cloud, a situation intensified by a misunderstanding in Aristotle about what interest is. Christian theologians over the course of centuries gradually came to understand more fully both new economic realities and the intent of Scriptural teaching, so that they were able to distinguish between fundamentally different types of lending situations (for example, lending to individuals for mere subsistence, versus lending to a merchant for a commercial enterprise).

The theologians of medieval and Renaissance Europe argued that it was immoral to charge interest on consumable goods like wheat, wine, and bread because the use of the thing could not be separated from its consumption. This teaching, they believed, upheld the clear admonition of Scripture to not exploit fellow Israelites in physically desperate circumstances, as when a poor farmer in Old Testament Israel would have to sell his children into indentured servitude to make ends meet. But many of these same theologians, following Aristotle, also considered money to be a good that could not be separated from its consumption. Money was considered to be sterile, and therefore taking interest on any loan—commercial or otherwise—was condemned, since all interest was regarded as "a breed of barren metal."

But this view of money as sterile began to change in the theological milieu of Spain after the year 1500, and by the end of the sixteenth century moral theologians all over Europe, Catholic and Protestant, were refining the basic understanding of interest that now prevails in modern economics[9]—that interest is the exchange ratio between different time horizons. If you prefer to save now, you must put off current consumption. This understanding opened the door for the recognition that many forms of lending at interest can be moral, so that the Church eventually condoned profit-making from money loaned (and therefore risked) in an entrepreneurial venture.[10]

Here's another way of putting "the exchange ratio between different time horizons": If you prefer to save now, you must put off current consumption. If I prefer to spend now, I must acquire the resources to do so. We can make an exchange between the money I want to spend and the money you want to save. You agree to lend me money, and we negotiate a fee to put to work what might otherwise have been idle resources. In doing so, of course, you as the lender cannot unilaterally dictate the terms because you must depend on my willingness to pay, and you must also compete with other lenders who may want my business. But neither can I, the borrower, simply declare what our bargain is worth without reference to you. The price we agree on for the loan is the interest rate. And different interest rates reflect the degree to which people prefer consumption over saving in different circumstances.

Naturally, people often complain about the high rates of interest on credit card debt, and legislation is often put forward to cap what credit card companies can charge, as if they were simply taking advantage of borrowers. But consider this: interest rates are only high if a balance is carried over from month to month. High interest rates discourage people from borrowing and putting off repayment—assuming of course that the credit card company is transparent about the interest rates and the person believes he will really have to pay the interest when push comes to shove.

The same principle holds true in general for interest rates—they encourage responsible behavior. Interest rewards those who save while it takes a fee from those who consume now. Not only that—they manage to do so on a sliding scale, so that the more you save, the more you are rewarded and the more you borrow, the more you are expected to pay for the privilege. The seemingly technical tool of the interest rate serves to train our moral dispositions, encouraging us to think about our responsibilities both now and in the future.[11]

Should mercy temper justice when it comes to lending, borrowing, and setting interest rates? Of course. And mercy is already baked into our nation's laws about loans and interest. Think about it. When a person defaults on a loan in our society, he is no longer flogged, killed, or sold into slavery. If his default on the loan wasn't willfully fraudulent, he won't even be thrown into prison. He will face consequences involving his credit, and he may be required to continue paying back some portion of the loan, but a whole system of mercy—modern bankruptcy law—stands between him and any lender who might want to suck a debtor dry or get revenge for his failure to repay.

It's no exaggeration to say that if some economic planner had set out to devise a system that encourages responsible thinking about the future, and discourages people from living for today without regard to the future, such a planner could not have devised a tool as effective as the interest rate. What is intriguing is that the interest rate isn't constructed by any person or group. It is an integral and deeply organic outgrowth of free economic relationships. It is part of the structure of economic reality and does not require a social consensus or a decision by a central board to bring it into being.

Consider for a moment what the consequences would be if legislation were enacted that set a low ceiling on how much interest companies could charge. Would we expect the amount of borrowing to increase or decrease? It is a simple matter of supply and demand: more credit will be purchased at a lower price than a higher price, all other things being equal. The result would be the buildup of more debt, the shortening of cultural time horizons, and the overall encouragement of irresponsibility. In other words, attempts to manipulate the interest rate would actually end up short-circuiting the moral training that the natural interest rate would otherwise bring about. This example may sound overly theoretical. In fact, I've just described a major component of the financial crisis that came to a head in 2008.

Through its control of the lending institutions Freddie Mac and Fannie Mae, the U.S. Federal Reserve held interest rates artificially low with the noble intention of encouraging banks (home lenders) to lend to borrowers (home buyers) they would not have otherwise lent to. The crisis was further worsened by the fact that the lending became politically driven. A free economy of borrowers and lenders didn't create the housing collapse. Government interventions in the marketplace did. Moral hazards created by government manipulations debased the culture of mortgage lending. And when the inevitable disaster arrived, Washington's answer was to impose *more* government interventions on the lending market—which was a bit like putting the weasel in charge of the henhouse he had just ransacked. Today, the U.S. government owns or guarantees the majority of mortgages in the United States—and more than 90 percent of new mortgages.[12] Where people are free to own and use property, tyranny can never hold sway. When people begin to sacrifice the rights of property and exchange—their economic freedom—for some other perceived good such as security or equality, they take a step down Hayek's road to serfdom. The lesson of history is plain. People who value political and religious liberty will ignore the value of economic liberty only at their peril.

Suggestions for Further Reading

Lord Acton, *The History of Freedom*, Parts I and II, available online at http://www.acton.org/research/history-freedom-antiquity and http://www.acton.org/research/history-freedom-christianity.

The Birth of Freedom Documentary (Acton Media, 2008). Further information available online at http://www.thebirthoffreedom.com/.

Cardinal Avery Dulles, "John Paul II and the Truth about Freedom," *First Things*, August/September 1995, http://www.firstthings.com/article/2008/09/004-john-paul-ii-and-the-truth-about-freedom-26.

Daniel Griswold, *Mad About Trade: Why Main Street America Should Embrace Globalization* (Cato Institute, 2009).

Dignitatis Humanae (Vatican II's Declaration on Religious Liberty), available at http://www.vatican.va/archive/hist_councils/ii_vatican_council/documents/vat-ii_decl_19651207_dignitatis-humanae_en.html.

Gilbert Meilaender, *Neither Beast nor God: The Dignity of the Human Person* (Encounter Books, 2009).

Michael Novak, *The Spirit of Democratic Capitalism* (Madison Books, 1990).

Index of Economic Freedom (annual editions), two versions available online, one at the Heritage Foundation, http://www.heritage.org/index/default, and one at the Fraser Institute, http://www.freetheworld.com/reports.html.

Rodney Stark, *The Victory of Reason* (Random House, 2005).

George Weigel, *The Cube and the Cathedral* (Basic Books, 2005).

CHAPTER 3

Want to Help the Poor? Start a Business

Q: Capitalism works great for America, but there are millions of poor people in the world who will never just pull themselves up by their bootstraps. Don't they need our help? Isn't that what charity and government-directed foreign aid are for?

■ ■ ■

A: There will always be a need for charity. But the one thing that is absolutely proven to raise people out of poverty isn't charity or foreign aid; it's the free market, and especially businesses that call on the capacities of the poor to create wealth, instead of addressing only their needs.

■ ■ ■

Seminaries are designed to get future priests to confront hard questions and difficult situations. When I was studying in Washington, D.C., part of our seminary formation involved us in various types of pastoral ministry. For a time I worked for the chaplain's office at the National Institutes of Health in Bethesda, often ministering to AIDS patients who were on an experimental drug that later came to be known as AZT.

During one of those semesters I was assigned to work in a soup kitchen run by a Catholic sister out of the basement of a Baptist church in the Anacostia area of D.C. The job called for my classmate and me to set up the chairs, serve the food, talk with those who came for a meal, and clean up afterward every Friday. The policy of this hard-working religious sister was "Whosoever will, may come." She meant that we were to serve anyone who showed up, no questions asked. At the time, her policy struck me as unambiguously wise. It was charitable, generous, and intended to do good to as many in the neighborhood as possible. The policy even resonated with Scripture. "Let him who is thirsty come," the book of Revelation says, "let him who desires take the water of life without price." Wasn't this what we were trying to do—in our own modest way, imitating what would be true in the hereafter?

The soup kitchen was even more than a transfer of material goods. We usually sat and ate with some of the lunch visitors, and it was during this time that I came to know people by their names and learned a little about them. It was a spiritually enriching and morally satisfying experience.

But I soon learned that it wasn't the whole story. One day my seminarian classmate and I had not eaten at the soup kitchen, and so after we cleaned up we decided to visit a fish-n-chips shop in the neighborhood.

When we arrived there was no one in the restaurant except a young girl cleaning tables, the cook, and the proprietor behind the cash register who took our order. As we sat down with our drinks awaiting our meal, a thought crossed my mind that frightened me. I was scared to express it to my classmate. It seemed a heretical thought, especially in light of all the obvious good we were doing at the soup kitchen just a few blocks away. But here was a family trying to run a small business. My best guess was that they lived nearby, and probably had saved up sufficient funds to open this shop only with great sacrifices. Maybe they had taken out a second mortgage on their house to do it. Their business required monthly payments for the rent, the lights, the food, water bills, heating bills, insurance, taxes, wages—the list could go on and on. And it struck me: we were this family's competitors!

And not just any competitors. We had distinct advantages over the fish-n-chips shop. At the soup kitchen we had none of these risks or bills: We owed no rent (the Baptist church gave us the use of the basement). We paid no wages (the soup kitchen was fully staffed by volunteers). We were responsible for no insurance payments, no utility bills, no taxes. Even the food we served was donated by ladies' church groups in Chevy Chase, Georgetown, and elsewhere. And the price at which we were offering the food was very competitive; meals at the soup kitchen were free.

I hesitated to tell my classmate what I was thinking, but then I tentatively tossed it out there.

He would have none of it. "But we're feeding the hungry who don't have the money to go here for lunch," he said.

Now that the discussion was on, I dove in. "How do we know?" I asked. "We take whoever comes. We never ask people anything."

As I sat there thinking through this, I realized that the problem ran even deeper. "Come to think of it," I said, "we never ask them *for* anything. There is no donation basket out. We never ask if they want to help prepare the food or help clean up. Other than feeding them and a little chitchat over lunch, we do not personally engage these people at all. We have no idea what their resources are—either monetary or personal. We just presume they have nothing to offer."

There was an uncomfortable silence as we waited for our lunch to be served. After the server brought our fish and chips, I began to feel a little bad about unloading on our well-intentioned soup kitchen. As we worked our way through the gloriously greasy meal, I tried feebly to turn the focus away from the soup kitchen and back onto the little restaurant. "I just hate to think we are making life more difficult for this family."

I don't remember what my friend said at that point. It was the last conversation we had on the topic, and yet for me it marked a turning point, or at least a deepening in my thinking about charity. Human beings are rich and complex entities, packed with all kinds of talents, dreams, foibles, and failings. And what I was coming to realize is that all too often policy planners and even religious people unwittingly allow themselves to be guided by a kind of materialist framework for helping the poor. We too often see them mostly as mouths and not as makers, as a locus of material needs rather than as creative beings packed with energy and capacity. It's a realization that has stayed with me ever since and guided everything I do in fighting poverty. Once you see poor people as bringing resources (not just needs) to the table, your whole view of how to help them changes.

This is why the Acton Institute, when exploring ways to help the poor, doesn't even start with the question, "What causes poverty?" Instead we ask, "What causes wealth?"

Jobs: The Best Anti-Poverty Program

Here is the simple reality: the past 200 years have seen the astounding rise of billions of the world's population out of abject poverty. But that in itself is not the astonishing thing. The amazing fact is that this has been accomplished not by charitable endeavors, much less by governmental aid programs. What rescued hundreds of millions of people from the direst poverty? Simple, humdrum business.

I am not saying that government policy and religious culture are unimportant in generating a climate in which businesses can thrive. And I am not saying there aren't legitimate concerns about the political and moral effects of globalization. What I am saying is that the process that lifted these billions of human beings out of poverty during the last two centuries, and particularly in the last fifty years, wasn't charity or public aid. Charitable efforts are vital expressions of human solidarity that, when carried out wisely, play a crucial role in relieving human suffering. But they are not the usual way people escape poverty. The normal way people rise out of poverty is through enterprise and markets—through ordinary business.

The data are incontrovertible: where people are free to pursue enterprise and connect to regional and global markets, the economy develops and great masses of people rise out of poverty. It may not be politically correct to point this out, but the reality is as plain as the pattern of lights that appears in satellite maps of the earth at night. Lights show mostly where geographical features encourage trade—around navigable rivers, lakes, and oceans. But the lights also tend to be where economic freedom allows entrepreneurs to purse wealth-generating enterprise. The example of North and South Korea—noted at the beginning of this book—offers a stark contrast: a single country separated by two radically different systems. The one in the south, despite its imperfections, is far more respectful of enterprise and basic human rights, while the one to the north is militantly opposed to economic, political, and religious freedom—and, for that matter, freedom of any kind. One sits quite literally in darkness. The other in light. The one breeds poverty. The other has moved millions of its people from poverty to prosperity.

We could extend these comparisons around the globe and back in time and come up with the same lesson: where there is economic freedom, poor countries tend to move from poverty to prosperity; where there is not, they don't. With the right conditions and incentives in place, people take initiative and the market expands. As workers specialize, efficiencies resulting from the division of labor allow greater productivity, and wealth grows. People acquire greater and greater chances to succeed at something they are good at and enjoy doing. The result is that between 1800 and 1950 the proportion of the world's population living in dire poverty halved, and from 1950 to 1980 it halved again.[1] In our time, many of the world's least fortunate experience material convenience and comfort on a scale undreamt of by the wealthiest elite of earlier centuries. Poverty still exists, much of it in countries ruled by corrupt, totalitarian regimes bent on suffocating human freedom. But such places are themselves a negative illustration of the wider pattern: Economic freedom and business enterprise lift people out of poverty; the absence of freedom and enterprise traps people in poverty.

The Fallacy of the Fixed Pie

What's even more remarkable is that all of this has occurred during a time when the world population has mushroomed from 1 billion people to 7 billion people. The fact that agricultural productivity has increased to feed these multitudes is only one part of the equation. As a proportion of the population, there are fewer farmers now than in 1900. What is everyone else doing? Many are producing the goods and offering the services that are needed to make life ever more convenient and comfortable. They are discovering ways of healing and sustaining life. They are inventing new methods of doing the usual things more quickly and efficiently, carving out leisure time for devotion to intellectual, physical, and spiritual pursuits that enhance human existence. Such advances are possible only because of the dynamism of the market economy and the businesses that make it go.

Many people miss the extraordinary power and value of ordinary business because—while far from being card-carrying Marxists—they have nevertheless inherited Marx's understanding of business and markets, usually without even realizing it. Marx portrayed economies as zero-sum games, particularly when it came to the relationship between those with invested capital and the workers these capitalists employed. I mean, really—Marx just didn't spend a whole lot of time celebrating the wealth-generating efforts of the entrepreneur or skilled manager. In his analysis, if anyone was creating new wealth, it was the poor laboring stiffs down in the trenches baking the bricks or planting the crops, not the rich guys in the offices who never broke a sweat. And if these fat cats relaxing in their offices got a bigger piece of the pie, then the laborers were bound to get a smaller piece. For Marx the capitalist class, the bourgeoisie, didn't create any wealth. They just skimmed some of the profits off of the laboring class's profitable labor. This fixed-pie analysis misses the fact that entrepreneurs grow the pie of wealth through their ideas and their orchestration of material and immaterial resources.

Think about it. The developing world is filled with hard-working people, every day many of them performing long hours of backbreaking labor that would send a highly fit professional athlete weeping to his mother! And yet they're still poor. What's missing from these contexts isn't manual labor or a good work ethic. What's missing are the entrepreneurs and the economic freedom necessary to channel all of this human energy into more efficient, creative, and productive labor.

It's easy for politicians to miss this fact because politics *is* a zero-sum game where the object is to divide up a static amount of pre-existing power and goods. The phenomenon of lobbying is a great instance of this because it is little more than a parasite on expansive government. Lobbyists only lobby those who have the power to influence things that will affect those they represent. If that power is curtailed, the lobbying makes no sense. No one lobbies me for corn subsidies because I don't have the power to give it to them. Success in the political system is based not on economic prowess but on political acumen.

Markets are very different. Consider the difference in atmosphere when you walk into a Hallmark card shop versus a post office. The incentives for advancement in government occupations are not the same as those for achieving success in private enterprise. The market is not a zero-sum game. Markets are dynamic; they grow; the people who work in them aim to please the customer, not the power holder.

In a market economy where the rule of law is enforced, businesses don't thrive by robbing others. They are successful when they have the foresight to anticipate the wants and needs of others and provide goods and services to customers at prices they are willing to pay. Apple didn't grow into a multi-billion dollar company by cleverly ripping off its customers. Amazon didn't grow into one of the biggest shippers of Christmas presents by putting coal in people's stockings. Everyone talks about the Enrons and Qwests of the corporate world, but in a vibrant market economy, crooked businesses are the exceptions, not the rule. If they were the rule, the United States would never have grown rich.

It may be an over-used slogan, but it's true: the market is a "win-win" proposition. It provides incentives for people to serve each other. I don't hand money over to my local grocer because I want him to win and me to lose. We make the exchange because it's a win-win deal. If it were a win-lose proposition, then the loser would stay home.

In politics, the pie is fought over to determine who gets what portion of the pie; in the market, the pie can grow.

Again, any system run by fallen human beings is going to have problems. Greed is a vice that tempts businesspeople, just as it tempted functionaries in the Soviet Union, clerics in medieval France, and imperial officers in ancient Rome. The material abundance that capitalism produces does carry with it the possibility that people may begin to identify with what they possess instead of who they are. The never-ending quest to "keep up with the Joneses" can become an addiction that leads to overwork, neglect of family, profligate spending, and crushing debt. But these dangers—what some call consumerism—are not unique to capitalist economies. Wealth acquired in other ways besides capitalism is at least as corrupting—consider the lives of aristocrats through the ages, or of oil potentates in today's Middle East. We cannot let the fear of our own moral failings in the face of material abundance lead us to embrace views and policies that will cut off millions of our brothers and sisters from climbing out of destitution. We cannot let our own mishandling of wealth condemn others to poverty.

My challenge to those who insist that the dangers and imperfections of capitalism outweigh its benefits is this: move to a remote and primitive village, untouched by the purported evils of a market economy, and see how well you do in a place without the benefit of a global business community constantly looking for ways to meet customers' wants and needs at attractive prices. We really need to step back and take in the absurdity: how many enemies of business have sat around grousing about the evils of global capitalism in a Starbucks while surfing the internet on an iPad, sipping a Jamaican roast, and wearing designer clothing that all came to them compliments of a global business economy?

Religious leaders are especially vulnerable to the prejudice against business, and a few years ago it occurred to me why this may be the case. Consider how most of us pastors come in touch with the money to run our churches and charitable institutions. We pass the basket and then "redistribute" the money to pay the bills. Now, there is nothing wrong with passing the basket. The problem is when pastors do not ask themselves where the money that went into the basket came from in the first place.

The expression "to make money" is a very good description of the process in a market. Things are traded, yes. Profits and losses are tallied up, yes. But it all begins, it is all sustainable, because people are making things; are creating things. It may be a product. It may be a service. It may be tangible. It may be intangible. But it all goes back to creation. Before the taking comes the making.

Foreign Aid That Doesn't

I've spent enough time traveling and speaking about these issues to realize that some people will hear all of this and nod but nevertheless feel that the wonders of capitalism in a developed economy like the United States are really beside the point when it comes to global poverty. The market economy works fine for the developed world, they say, but the economically weaker nations of the world need a helping hand. The best way to do this, the argument goes, is for the governments of wealthy nations to infuse development dollars into poor nations so that they can fund the infrastructure projects necessary to whip their economies into competitive form.

It sounds good, but fifty years of experience suggest that it simply doesn't work. Government-to-government aid—the conventional method—has an unfortunate tendency to get into the wrong hands; as British development economist Peter Bauer once put it, "foreign aid is a process by which poor people in rich countries help rich people in poor countries."[2] Dumping money into political situations where corruption is rampant does not promote genuine economic development. Instead it often perpetuates the dysfunctional political and moral cultures that have kept the country's people in poverty.

That isn't just the assessment of a few middle class economists from the West. An increasing number of experts from the developing world have come to recognize the pitfalls of government-to-government aid. The Acton Institute has come into contact with many of these innovative thinkers through our work on the PovertyCure initiative, an effort to rethink the issues of global poverty, international aid, and business. Part of a growing movement of market-friendly reformers, the PovertyCure network and website—www.povertycure.org—emphasize that what poor nations need is not aid money from foreign governments, but instead the freedom to unleash the creativity inherent in their own communities. The world's poor need businesses that will enable them to lift their societies out of poverty, not just crumbs from our table. Many people in these developing countries don't fear the challenges of the market; they embrace them and are pleading with wealthy countries to stop walling them out of various markets. Rwandan President Paul Kagame is a controversial figure, but in an interview with the Acton Institute in Kigali in the fall of 2008, he articulated well an increasingly common sentiment among Africans. "Competition helps bring out everybody's potential," he said. "And it doesn't matter what level of society. Even the poor people have that energy, deserve that freedom where they can be able to compete with the rest, and do the best they can."[3]

When the people in developing countries are given the economic freedom to compete in the marketplace, the term "developing economy" quickly ceases to be a euphemism and becomes a reality. In Peru, Aquilino Flores, struggling to make ends meet by washing cars, began selling t-shirts. Flores noticed the opportunity because he understood his customers' needs and the culture of the local workers. His business grew into a textile and clothing multinational that now provides jobs for five thousand people. He exports goods worth tens of millions of dollars annually, and because his workers can now afford more goods and services, the local economy is enriched.[4]

Unfortunately, would-be entrepreneurs like Flores are often blocked from putting their imagination and hard work to use. Bureaucratic regulation and a corrupt political culture makes starting a legal business virtually impossible for people in many parts of the world. In his book *The Mystery of Capital*, the internationally respected development economist Hernando de Soto describes in tragicomic detail the almost surreal amount of red tape and bureaucracy a poor person in the developing world usually has to go through to obtain a business license.

De Soto notes that when he began investigating this in the early '80s, all of the big law firms he consulted in Peru assured him that setting up a formal business to get access to investment capital would be quick and easy. De Soto knew that was probably true for him, but what about for somebody living in a shantytown without political connections? He and his colleagues decided to test the question by establishing a two-sewing-machine shirt-making business in a Lima shantytown, and he took himself out of the equation by sending out four students under the supervision of a seasoned lawyer to do the work of trying to comply with all of the legal requirements. "I've discovered that to become legal took more than three hundred days, working six hours a day," De Soto writes. "The cost: thirty-two times the monthly minimum wage."[5]

That's not a path. That's not a free market. That's a wall, an unscalable barrier that locks the poor out of the formal business sector and protects the well-connected. What de Soto realized is that the poor don't need more foreign handouts so much as they need a better, more streamlined legal system for starting formal businesses, a system that encourages aspiring entrepreneurs instead of suffocating them. De Soto's Institute for Liberty and Democracy (ILD) has been promoting such reforms in Peru and in other developing countries ever since.

And it's not just that free goods shipped as aid fail to address the lack of economic freedom among the poor in the developing world. As counterintuitive as it may be, the free goods themselves in fact make it harder for people in "the developing world" to actually develop their economies. Everywhere we travel in the developing world we hear discouraging stories about businesses and whole industries decimated by the free shipments of goods from public and private charity coming from Western countries.

In Kenya, for instance, entrepreneur Eva Muraya talked to us in March 2011 about the present cotton and apparel industries in her country today versus when she was growing up. "When I was growing up, we didn't have secondhand clothing sold in Kenya," she said. "My mother took me to a store, and she bought me a beautiful t-shirt that said, 'Made in Kenya,' 'Kenya Cotton.' Today, I would struggle to find a t-shirt like that for my daughter. Why? Because of the influx of secondhand clothing in the late '70s and early '80s. The secondhand clothing that makes its way here from Europe and the U.S. and Canada, has negatively impacted our textile industry in Kenya—massive layoffs in the '80s and the '90s, factories that shut down.... What happened to our cotton farms? When I was growing up in this country, we could have bought cotton in varieties and types that are incomparable. But that's all gone, because of the impact, the negative impact, of the apparel inputs at a secondhand level."[6]

We heard similar stories in the Caribbean. In Haiti we spoke with the founders of Enersa, an indigenous technology company specializing in the manufacturing, installation, and maintenance of solar power,[7] a source of energy that is competitive there without government subsidies because of the plentiful sunshine and lack of an electrical infrastructure in many areas. Enersa was growing and thriving, but then they almost went under in the months after the 2010 earthquake, not so much because the quake damaged their factory as because almost none of the outside aid groups who wanted to provide free solar panel technology bothered to find out if there were any local suppliers providing it at competitive prices and with the advantage of local knowledge.

Fortunately, Enersa survived and is again thriving, but not all of the stories of this sort have a happy ending. Haiti's rice farmers, for instance, have been decimated by subsidized U.S. rice dumped on the country as free aid. Creating a surplus of rice in the United States by subsidizing it and then buying the extra to ship it as aid may be good politics in rice-producing states like Arkansas, but it's a disaster for farmers in developing countries who find themselves having to compete against free goods.

Even President Bill Clinton, who supported food aid to Haiti during his tenure in the White House, called the policy into question during testimony before the Senate Committee on Foreign Relations in March 2010. "It may have been good for some of my farmers in Arkansas, but it has not worked. It was a mistake," he said. "I had to live everyday with the consequences of the loss of capacity to produce a rice crop in Haiti to feed those people because of what I did."[8]

What is it exactly that President Clinton did? Some would say he pushed free markets on Haiti, and that was the problem, since Haiti's rice production further eroded after the United States pressured the island nation to lower its tariffs on rice imports. The problem with this line of reasoning is that it assumes the U.S.-Haiti rice market actually became free after the tariffs were lowered. It didn't. The United States was heavily subsidizing U.S. rice imports into Haiti both before and after the tariffs were lowered. Drawing from multiple sources, Timothy Schwartz reports that from 1986 to 2000, the United States was subsidizing corn, wheat, cotton, and rice at about 38 percent a year.[9] Haiti's local rice farming was decimated not by free markets but by heavily subsidized markets, by an insider's game of the well-connected—in this case, U.S. politicians and some mostly very large corporate farms in states like Arkansas. If pursuing policies that genuinely help the poor to flourish is really our intention, it's high time we stopped confusing free market capitalism with big government cronyism.

The good news is that many people in high places genuinely do want to help the poor. In their case it's mainly a matter of helping them understand the importance of economic freedom. The bad news is that we cannot always count on intentions to be pure as the driven snow. As Schwartz has noted in his book *Travesty in Haiti* and in our PovertyCure interview with him in early 2012, the United States global food aid program, begun in 1954 as Public Law 480, was never primarily about helping the poor. This claim may strike many as implausibly cynical. But Schwartz points out that USAID's own website boasted of U.S. government food aid as a means of expanding U.S. agricultural exports into developing countries. The point is fairly muted on USAID's website as it appeared in early 2012, but if you troll the internet archives to view the website as it appeared a decade ago, the point comes through more strongly. Here, for instance, is a USAID web page from the year 2000 trumpeting the "Direct Economic Benefits of U.S. Assistance by State":

> The principal beneficiary of America's foreign assistance programs has always been the United States. Close to 80 percent of the U.S. Agency for International Development's (USAID's) contracts and grants go directly to American firms. Foreign assistance programs have helped create major markets for agricultural goods, created new markets for American industrial exports and meant hundreds of thousands of jobs for Americans.[10]

There would be nothing wrong with increasing exports from the United States to the developing world if that trade took place in a really free market. That would be a truly win-win situation for Americans and our trading partners. But government subsidies to American agriculture mean that the exchange between us and them is anything but free and equal. Such government spending doesn't actually help the overall U.S.

economy; it enriches farmers having political clout at the expense of both the poor in the developing world and other American citizens. But here let's keep our focus on what the passage from the USAID website illustrates: the motivations behind much of Washington's government-to-government aid programs are far from altruistic. This is common knowledge in the aid industry; it's one reason that so many people in the developing world have grown sick of aid. This doesn't mean that rich countries can do nothing useful *vis-à-vis* poor countries. It just means we need to rethink development. The place to start is to look for things that correlate strongly with actual economic development—such as was achieved by the Western world in the past few centuries—and focus efforts in that direction.

The table below from the World Bank, 2011, underscores the remarkable correlation between business environment and prosperity. Where people are free to plant and grow businesses, material betterment readily follows. Where they are discouraged from doing so, material deprivation is the result.

Ease of Doing Business Index[11]

Top 10 MOST Business-Friendly Countries	Top 10 LEAST Business-Friendly Countries
1. Singapore	1. Chad
2. Hong Kong SAR, China	2. Central African Republic
3. New Zealand	3. Congo, Rep.
4. United States	4. Eritrea
5. Denmark	5. Guinea
6. Norway	6. Congo, Dem. Rep.
7. United Kingdom	7. Venezuela, RB
8. Korea, Rep.	8. Guinea-Bissau
9. Iceland	9. Benin
10. Ireland	10. Haiti

Notice the pattern? It's hard to miss. The countries with high levels of economic freedom are economically rich or on the way to growing rich. The countries that are famously business-unfriendly are mired in poverty. Free stuff won't solve the problems of that second group. Freedom will.

What then can wealthy nations do to assist developing countries? First, don't make the matter worse by encouraging corruption and governmental irresponsibility, which is exactly what government-to-government aid tends to do. Second, stop undercutting businesses in the developing world by flooding their markets with free goods year after year. Save emergency aid for genuine emergencies, and when you rush in to help, see if there are any local producers already there with whom you can partner to source emergency provisions. Third, open the world's markets to the businesses of emerging economies. As things stand today, many Western nations practice the confused and contradictory policy of protecting domestic firms through tariffs and subsidies—thereby shutting out the products of developing nations—and at the same time sending billions of dollars in tax money to developing nations to supplement their failing economies. This is the misguided strategy we have used to "develop" Haiti for the past few decades. Is it any wonder Haiti's people are still struggling to develop?

Rather than undercut local businesses with an endless stream of free goods, private charitable groups can render genuine long-term assistance by encouraging reforms so that ethical businesses can flourish: they can promote transparency and democracy in government, educate and train in both technical skills and the virtuous habits necessary for commercial success, and support business activity among the poor through either traditional investment instruments or special methods such as microloans.

Pope Benedict makes a rather intriguing suggestion in his encyclical *Caritas in Veritate*, where he raises the idea of what he calls "fiscal subsidiarity"—by which he means permitting citizens to take a portion of their tax liability (perhaps some of the funds presently used for government-to-government aid) and redirect it as investments directly to developing nations. The proposal is worth a vigorous debate.[12]

For those of us with a genuine concern for the poorest of the poor, it's long past time for us to rethink poverty relief. Even before the earthquake in Haiti, there were some ten thousand NGOs doing charitable work there, most of them in close connection with one or more governments from the developed world, to dispense top-down paternalistic aid. They were there before the earthquake. They remain there after the earthquake. What also remains in Haiti is the sense of hopelessness and resentment among many Haitians that they will never control their own national and personal destinies again.

If traditional top-down aid were the solution, Haiti would be among the fastest developing poor countries in the world, since it has received a flood of aid for decades. But as many in the developing world have been tactfully or not so tactfully trying to tell the West for many years now, that kind of aid is not the solution. Rwandan Anglican Bishop John Rucyahana put it gently when he told us, "We are no longer getting excited by aid." Ghanaian software developer Herman Chinery-Hesse, who has been called "the Bill Gates of Africa," was blunter in his interview with us. "I have never heard of a country that developed on aid," he said. "If you know of one, just let me know. I know about countries that developed on trade and innovation and business. I don't know of any country that got so much aid that it suddenly became a first world country. I've never heard of such a country. So the track is wrong; that track ends to nowhere."[13]

The Moral Appeal of Good Work

The aid question runs deeper than how and where we direct money. As we plan and execute our political and charitable endeavors, we need to be mindful of the danger of inadvertently discouraging human initiative generally and entrepreneurs specifically—after all, they are the builders of the businesses that will supply the means to feed, clothe, and shelter the world's people. The renowned twelfth-century rabbi Moses Maimonides put it succinctly when he said, "Anticipate charity by preventing poverty." For Maimonides, creating independence in a poor person was the highest level of charity.[14] When companies create jobs, opportunities for economic advancement abound. Struggling men and women who obtain jobs not only better their own situation. Through their work they also contribute to the goods and services available in a community's economy. This process is sustainable in a way that charitable assistance is not. The creation and attainment of gainful employment ends the vicious cycle of dependency and starts a virtuous cycle of participation in the market economy. Jobs are the world's best antipoverty program.

A Theology of Enterprise

This makes economic sense. It also makes theological sense. The creative dimension of work in the market economy suggests that business, far from being a necessary evil—as some of my fellow pastors tend to view it—can instead be a positive calling or vocation. The very first recorded words of God to the newly created human family in the book of Genesis bear on this. The backdrop to these words is the account of the six days of creation. God is seen acting as a kind of grand impresario, forming and making things and pronouncing them good (cf. Genesis 1:1–28). On the sixth day God finally fashions humanity from "the dust of the earth" and infuses into humankind "the breath of life."

At this point in the narrative, the author of Genesis describes man and woman as being created "in the image of God" ("*imago Dei*"). To be made in the image of God is to be like Him in His creative capacity. God invokes this creativity with His first words to Adam and Eve: "Be fruitful and multiply." The command can be seen as extending beyond the procreative action of childbearing to all that human beings do to provide for themselves and others. Work is given to humanity as a vocation or calling, not as a curse, since the pair was instructed to cultivate the garden before the fall. It was only after sin entered the picture that work descended into toil and man was told that he must work by the "sweat of your face" (Genesis 3:19). But this was not the original nature of the vocation to work, and although the toilsome quality of work persists in many ways, it also represents a path to personal fulfillment, service to others, and cooperation in God's plan for the world. This is why it is such an offense against human dignity when people are prevented from expressing their creative initiative, when they are enslaved or hindered in discovering some specific vocation God has equipped them for in this world. This is exactly what happens when individuals are prevented by the kind of artificial limitations that freeze out the up-and-comers and protect insiders, or when existing businesses are discouraged—by an uncertain political environment, an unpredictable or inequitable system of laws, or burdensome labor regulations—from generating new jobs.

The economic and the moral dimensions of the issues that face us today are interconnected. Employment for those in need may seem like mainly an economic or financial matter, but it is much more than that. C. Neal Johnson, a business professor and former missionary, visited Grand Rapids recently, and in an interview for our PovertyCure initiative, he described the plight of unemployment in all its facets in Kazakhstan as it struggled to move out from under the shadow of its Soviet past:

> The men were out, they didn't think well of themselves so what did they do? They turned to the bottle; alcoholism problems were really rampant. They're angry, they're frustrated, they have no hope in life, and they don't see any value in their life. But you take that same person, you give them a job, you give them something meaningful, and it can totally change their attitude toward life and give them hope, give them promise.

Neal is not a traditional missionary. He is encouraging what is called "Business as Mission," a strategy and calling of being salt and light in developing regions by founding businesses that are run with a commitment to excellence and virtue. For the poor of Kazakhstan, he insists, "Business not only creates valuable goods and services," but the employment those businesses supply gives people "a whole different sense of who they are, what their purpose is, and what their hope is for the future. And the social implications of that are just enormous."[15]

The message of this chapter is a hopeful one. The poorest countries of the world are filled with needs, many of them heartbreaking. But they are also filled with creatures made in the image of God, human beings filled with energy and capacity. The countries that have found ways of unleashing that creativity through economic freedom have lifted millions out of poverty. What works, it seems, is work—creative, entrepreneurial, and free.

Suggestions for Further Reading

Peter Bauer, *From Subsistence to Exchange* (Princeton University Press, 2000).

Philip Booth, *International Aid and Integral Human Development* (Acton Institute, 2011).

The Call of the Entrepreneur Documentary (Acton Media, 2007). Further information available online at http://www.calloftheentrepreneur.com/.

Paul Collier, *The Bottom Billion* (Oxford University Press, 2008).

R. Glenn Hubbard and William Duggan, *The Aid Trap: Hard Truths About Ending Poverty* (Columbia Business School Publishing, 2009).

PovertyCure website (www.povertycure.org).

Robert Sirico, *The Entrepreneurial Vocation* (Acton Institute, 2001).

CHAPTER 4

Why the "Creative Destruction" of Capitalism Is More Creative than Destructive

Q: It's easy to talk about "creative destruction" when it's not your job, your family, or your town being destroyed. Unemployment ruins lives. Shouldn't we do all we can to have less of it? Shouldn't the government and unions protect workers from losing their jobs?

■ ■ ■

A: Ironically, a truly free labor market *is* the way to have less unemployment. We must assist the individuals who are hurt by the economy's growing pains. But if we attempt to prevent unemployment by making it difficult to let people go, more people will suffer in the stagnation that such regulations force on the economy.

■ ■ ■

As I pulled into the driveway of the house my religious community lives in, I was horrified to see that all the green holly bushes surrounding the front and side of the house had been decimated. Entering the house, I saw Fr. James washing up from some strenuous labor.

I asked him what happened to the holly bushes.

"I cut them back," he replied.

"*You* did that? Why did you kill them?"

"I didn't kill them," was his reply. "I pruned them. If you want them to be healthy for next year, it is important that they not dissipate their energy to the more extended branches. If we let the branches go, they would threaten the entire bush and we'd have nothing."

Fr. James is a born and bred Midwesterner. I grew up in Brooklyn, and I was out of my depth. What he was saying made sense to me on a technical level, but all my intuitions cried out against it. It looked horrible.

Creative Destruction, Creative Flourishing

I relate this story as an illustration of the fact that sometimes what appears to be beaten back and damaged is really healthy and preparing for new growth. This is the case with what economists call *creative destruction*—the phenomenon whereby old skills, companies, and sometimes entire industries are eclipsed as new methods and businesses take their place. Creative destruction is seen in layoffs, downsizing, the obsolescence of firms, and, sometimes, serious injury to the communities that depend on them. It looks horrible, and, especially when seen through the lives of the people who experience such economic upheaval, it can be heartrending. But think of the alternative—What if the American Founders had constructed a society where no industry was ever allowed to go under because it would mean a lot of innocent people losing their jobs? I mean, have you ever met a livery yard owner or a stable boy? How about a blacksmith or a farrier? Do you have among your acquaintances any makers of bridles, saddles, chaises, coaches, or buggy whips?

All of these once-booming forms of remunerative employment are either extinct or occupy tiny niches in today's economy. Their doom was sealed on October 1, 1908, when Henry Ford introduced the Model T—the culmination of a long period of experimentation and advance in automobile technology involving many inventors across many countries. All of these professions were tied to what had been to that point a primary means of land transportation over short distances (and over long, until the introduction of the railroad)—namely, the horse.

The transition from the horse to the automobile was painful for many farriers and saddle makers. As business waned, they would have experienced slowdowns and unemployment, unless and until they were able to adapt to the changing marketplace and find employment in new fields.

Keep in mind, too, that even in times of economic transition, the workers in trades that are becoming obsolete are not all affected in the same way. Those hurt the most are likely to be older workers who are reaching retirement at the same time the technology changes or other workers who for various reasons find themselves unable to add skills or retrain. Most workers, however, will find employment; for them it's a matter of temporary dislocation. Some will even find work closely related to their previous occupation. It is not as though every ditch digger is going to lose his job when bulldozers come on line. Let's not forget the creative and progressive part of creative destruction. Technological advance does not destroy ditch diggers, even the ones who lose their jobs. It places them behind the controls of bulldozers or in factories building them, or nudges them into other fields that employ their brains as well as their brawn, since not as many ditch diggers are needed when the hands that wielded shovels are now running Caterpillar machines.

Those caught in the midst of such revolutions in production deserve our special attention and support. Employers can ease the transition by managing such change in ways that are conscientious and humane. Workers can be encouraged and assisted to retrain within a company. For those who cannot be retained, firms can make the experience less painful by providing adequate warning and a generous severance or early retirement package. Where companies are financially unable to help in these ways, or where such aid is not sufficient, religious and other charitable institutions can play an important role.

This is not wishful thinking. It is in many cases present reality. Many businesses do treat their employees well, and many charitable organizations do stand by ready to help people in need of employment assistance.

One of the programs affiliated with the Acton Institute is our Samaritan Awards, which has honored charities that do outstanding work with little or no government funding. Our top award winner several years ago was the Christian Women's Job Corps of Middle Tennessee, which promotes self-sufficiency via gainful employment among female ex-offenders and underemployed or unemployed women living in poverty.

But the question of whether and how to assist those injured by economic transitions is a very different question from whether the government should step in to halt such economic transitions. In the interest of preserving existing jobs and industries, should society have declared an end to progress in transportation technology and rested content with the horse and buggy? The efficiencies and economic productivity that widespread use of the internal combustion engine generated should be obvious. Transporting the teeming populations of modern cities would be impossible without these advances. Feeding them would be unthinkable without the leaps in agricultural productivity that were made possible, in part, by mechanized farming.

And, yes, we need innovative people to continue the process of looking for better and better ways to minimize air and water pollution, but it is precisely the creative ferment of our free economy that has allowed us to make so many economically practical advances in this regard. More progress is possible, but let's be careful to compare the current situation with live alternatives. For those disturbed by the air pollution cars and trucks cause, imagine the filth that would pour down the streets of a New York or Los Angeles overcrowded with a few million horses, mules, and oxen. We can romanticize a city life of horse-drawn carriages because we don't have to smell or shovel or walk through the churned up mud and manure that characterized those cities for centuries. Instead, for us, the horse-drawn carriage is a novelty for a special summer evening downtown.

Here in Michigan, one of the jewels of the Great Lakes is Mackinac Island. There are no motorized vehicles there during the regular vacation season, at least not any that the tourists are allowed to see. It's an extraordinarily charming place with many touches from an age long vanished (and the fudge isn't bad either). But we need to recognize what this place is and what makes it possible. The prosperity from a free and industrialized economy creates sufficient surplus wealth to fund all of the labor and tools needed to make the motor-free island a fresh and clean vacation experience. It's not an accurate representation of what life was like for most people in an age of horse-drawn travel, and it probaby isn't intended to be.

We can enjoy such experiences. We can use our imaginations to appreciate the beautiful things from olden times. We can even mourn the evil and ugly uses that modern technology is sometimes put to. But we should not let a false nostalgia blind us to the good of human progress. If we were to eliminate the positive results of even a hundred years of creative destruction—eliminate them overnight—the result would be the swift death of literally billions of human beings, since the resources available to civilization a hundred years ago could not possibly feed, clothe, and medically treat even half of the planet's current population.

Billions of human lives would be lost, along with the access that billions of people now have to reading, education, music, and art, as well as the opportunity to develop and use many a particular talent that, in a previous age, would have had to "waste its sweetness on the desert air" because there was simply no outlet for the person's undiscovered capacity for, say, managing a design company, or programming software, or running complex, life-saving equipment in a hospital. We are blessed to live in an alternate reality, and if we are to preserve it we need to recognize that it is only when the process of creative destruction is allowed that new jobs, new skills, new ways of leveraging human energy can spring up and create the opportunities that previous generations never even realized were possible.

If our aim is to make progress toward the free and virtuous society, a fatuous nostalgia isn't going to help us. What is needed, rather, is an economically informed perspective. We need to look more closely at all the factors contributing to creative destruction, and consider both the positives and negatives of a creative market economy. That involves not only attending to the people thrown out of work as industries and technologies change but also thinking about what would happen to the people if there were no creative destruction.

Once we realize that we have to attend to all of the long-range consequences, then we can start coming at the problems generated by creative destruction from the most productive angle. The challenge for all who are concerned with promoting a free and virtuous society is to minimize the damage done to people by the economy's dynamism without suppressing that dynamism by wrapping business in a regulatory straitjacket. Sure, we could protect obsolete industries. But are you really protecting a person's dignity by enticing him to continue making an obsolete product? How would you like to look back on ten or twenty years of labor and know that it wasn't genuinely profitable but persisted only because your industry or business was on the public dole?

The problem goes beyond the loss of personal dignity. Every time resources are used to prop up an obsolete industry or inefficient company, those are resources that cannot be used to fuel profitable and sustainable industries and businesses. The more resources an economy routes into inefficient and obsolete industries and businesses, the less economic growth there is for the economy as a whole. If labor and skills are not allowed to shift from sector to sector to find their most highly valued use, then economic stagnation is the inevitable result. An economy that blocks such shifts locks in unproductive ventures and eventually stagnates—much like the holly bush that is never pruned.

Of course, workers and other economic players who are caught in the midst of this drama of creative destruction aren't landscape plants; they are human persons and members of families. Every job is filled by a human being of inestimable inherent dignity and worth. The truth is that there is a miniature moral drama behind every layoff and every business that fails. The unemployment data do not reveal the whole story. Behind the numbers reported by the media are the sufferings of individuals—their private doubts, confusion, upheaval, shame, desperation, and sometimes despair.

In my pastoral work, I have dealt with people whose concerns for the economic security of their families dwarf any other issues in their lives. Fathers who face a future without a paycheck ask fundamental questions about their own self-worth, while mothers who are laid off find themselves concerned about clothes, food, and even shelter for their children. Single men and women worry about downshifts in their social status and the prospects for their future.

Is it right that such momentous decisions concerning job security should generally be left to the vicissitudes of the commercial marketplace? My European friends find this prospect appalling. In France, Spain, Italy, and many other EU countries, the state imposes every manner of restriction on the right of employers to let workers go or to fire them outright. To cut someone from the payroll is viewed as an egregious act of cruelty, an act of exploitation from which the state must protect the working class. When someone is actually laid off or fired, most EU countries provide unemployment benefits that last up to two—in some places five—years, and deliver 60 to 90 percent of the net earnings from the last year of employment. All of this sounds gentle and loving, and many interest groups in the United States, particularly some labor unions, would like similar laws in this country. What they don't seem to realize is that benefits of these kinds naturally require steep taxes to support them and large agencies to administer them. Then navigating these byzantine bureaucracies involves an investment of time and energy equal to or surpassing that associated with job applications. As the recent debt crises in many European nations indicate, heavy taxation and job-killing regulation combined with lavish social spending eventually create an imbalance that is impossible to sustain. Even before the imbalance became acute, the heavy requirements imposed on entrepreneurs and employers led to stunted job creation and decades of chronically high unemployment rates.

By comparison, the United States has traditionally had a relatively free job market in which employers have discretion over layoffs and non-discriminatory firings. Until the extensions enacted after the recent downturn, unemployment benefits here were modest in comparison to those in Europe, usually lasting only about six months and only available under fairly restrictive conditions (laid off, not fired with cause; full time employee rather than a contract or part time employee).

What was the result of this supposedly mean-spirited system? Lower unemployment rates, faster job growth, and people being spurred to find and enter jobs where they could better use their talents to add value and earn a living. The U.S. system was the compassionate system. If you want to see mean, look what the welfare state in a country like Greece has done to its people.

How did the American approach, with fewer government benefits and protections, lead to a fairer, more flourishing outcome? On balance, a free market in labor leads to more opportunities for everyone and reflects a basic fairness inherent in a social order in which people are free to buy and sell labor without being forced into it—what Christian theologians refer to as "commutative justice." Just as an employee is free to leave an employer at any time, an employer is also free to decide whom he or she will continue to offer payment to in exchange for labor. If the two parties can agree on salary and job expectations, then they come together for a win-win exchange. If one party doesn't think he or she is winning in the economic exchange, that party is free to look elsewhere. Neither party is forced to do anything.

A free market in labor strikes many as heartless and cruel, but constricted, European-style labor markets mean more unemployment for more people and the production of fewer of the goods and services for everyone. Now, many people heartily approve of the worker being free to seek employment and leave employment as he so desires. But these same people see no reason to extend to the employer a similar freedom on his side of the relationship. What such people may not realize, at least not fully, is that workers are not the only ones forced by economic ups and downs to adjust to new challenges and opportunities. Businesses face these same challenges.

In a genuinely free economy, the typical relationship between employee and employer is not one of exploitation, as Marx would have it, but of mutual benefit. Free of coercion, the two parties cooperate in the service of the customer, the employer and employee functioning as mutual benefactors. If the arrangement becomes disagreeable, it is renegotiated, or one party severs the relationship. But in the most successful labor relationships, both parties are constantly aware of how the other benefits him and the whole relationship is marked by attitudes of humility and responsibility.

Barring interventions by regulators and union officials, workers negotiate their own terms of employment to their advantage. In boom times when jobs go begging, the employees have the advantage and can call forth higher wages. These higher wages not only benefit the employees, they serve the market function of attracting more workers to the profitable sectors, allowing them to grow and flourish to meet the increased market demand. In times of relative contraction, the pressure runs the other way, so that the employer is able to find suitably skilled workers without raising salaries. He may even tighten salaries. This allows the employer to stay profitable during the lean times, stay in business, and thereby continue to provide jobs for the economy.

When my European friends express astonishment that I would defend this system, I simply ask: Why would you want to work for a company that you know, in your heart of hearts, does not really want you working there because it can no longer afford to pay you? Why would you want to continue to be employed, not as an asset to a firm, but as a liability? Isn't it rather selfish to insist that someone pay you, not because you are providing them with the kind and amount of work that justifies that pay, but instead because they are under duress and fear the law?

To disallow employers to terminate employment compels them to keep a larger workforce than is required to achieve profitability—like threatening the entire holly bush by neglecting to trim the extended branch. That is to say, restrictions on the labor market impose losses on business. These losses are ultimately paid for down the line by the customers of the business, who may see higher prices, and by the workers, who may enjoy fewer benefits and wage increases—and possibly still lose their jobs in the end, if the business ceases to be sustainable.

Again, consider the alternative. A system of free labor gives workers a sense of their own value. They can be sure that every job they hold is a result of their own efforts, every paycheck a reflection of their own contribution to the community of work. Workers in a free economy see that their labor is part of a vast matrix of human cooperation and that, far from being a drain on society, the employees are making a meaningful contribution.

The U.S. system, supposedly more individualistic and less sensitive to social concerns, is actually more conducive to the common good. It encourages the individual worker to think about the good of the whole firm, because his or her fate in that particular job is tied to the welfare of the entire business. I've talked with business owners of unionized companies who can never quite get over their shock at realizing that some of their workers are willing to go so far as to kill the company in order to maximize their own pay and benefits in the short term, without any apparent regard for the effect on their co-workers or the consumers of their products. There is something fundamentally alarming about that.

To resist the creative destruction inherent in a dynamic economy is only to replace creative destruction with a slow destruction without creativity. This isn't theory. It's the present reality in the United States. For several years now, but particularly since 2008, our nation's political leaders have been pushing our country off of the road of economic freedom and onto a path away from the creativity and dynamism of a free economy in search of an illusory system of economic security and "fairness." The result has been moribund job creation, high unemployment, and a population wondering if it will ever be morning in America again.

The perfectly "safe" economy is the economy where nothing and no one face challenges and growth, but such an economy is not really safe at all because it is not a living, thriving economy. It's not an economy, moreover, worthy of men and women of inestimable dignity, worth, and capacity. Losing a job can be one of the most difficult events of a person's life, but it need not be the end of the road. It can mean accepting a lower salary, but it can also open up new opportunities that prove more fruitful in the future. Nor is one's time with any company or sector necessarily a bad investment. The job may not be lucrative or glamorous, but developing the habits associated with doing a job well is something no one can take from you. The athlete doesn't improve without effort and struggle, and what is true of the athlete is true of the human person and the human economy as a whole. Walling ourselves off from challenges, struggles, and setbacks is a recipe for decline.

Globalization, Christianity, and Culture

It is impossible to talk about creative destruction without talking about the increasingly interconnected global economy. The global economy is where we see creative destruction writ large, and in recent years many

Americans have had to come face to face with the destructive side of the global economy's creative ferment.

In the 1990s, the idea of globalization emerged in the popular consciousness as a new way of describing the interactions of human beings around the world—the contemporary reality of global economic integration and the impossibility of economic isolation. Basically, globalization means the increasing interconnectedness of all peoples on the face of the earth, a state of affairs that evokes high praise from some and bitter condemnation from others.

For Christians, rejecting globalization wholesale is a curious position at best. The universal message of the Christian Church, summarized perhaps most memorably in the Great Commission of Jesus at the end of the Gospel of Matthew, gave rise to the first truly global religion, one tied neither ideologically nor geographically to any particular country or empire. Historically, Christianity, in both its best and worst moments, has been intimately tied up in the historical process of globalization.

How does globalization affect the average American today? Globalization is inextricably linked to industrialization and the continuing discoveries afforded by the scientific revolution. We tend to conflate these change agents. However, if we allow ourselves to paint with broad brushstrokes, the resulting picture of globalization is one in which we can move more rapidly and cheaply, and thus share more of ourselves as well as our consumer goods with people near and far. A globalized planet is one in which our material and human capital, along with the values that compose our respective cultures can cross international borders with relative ease (though admittedly these values are not all equally desirable). This increasing ability to share our God-given and complementary gifts with one another holds out the possibility of enlarging the scope of our communion and solidarity.

Technology plays a role, but so too does a widely shared cultural conviction. The belief that all human beings have inherent dignity and worth, that they "are created equal," supports the shared conviction that people everywhere should be free from unreasonable constraints imposed by other persons or the state. In economics, globalization broadens markets to include many nations that were previously isolated one from another. One of the results is that citizens in countries with abusive regimes often gain access to information about what a life under political liberty looks like, and a wave of reform energy begins to transform the nation. Many people in the 1970s in the Soviet Union spoke about seeing Western tourists in jeans as giving them a window into a freer and more personally expressive world.

Meanwhile, the extension of the division of labor characteristic of globalization results in the reduction of costs for the things that people depend on for their well-being. It enables those in poorer regions of the world to participate more fully in what Pope John Paul II called the "circle of exchange," building an infrastructure of enterprise within their own countries, and with entrepreneurs in other countries, making people less dependent upon the whims of political rulers—foreign and domestic—for their well-being and economic progress.

Globalization and Coercive Destruction

Against all of the arguments for economic globalization stands the specter of the sweatshop—factories where the poor of the developing world are paid pennies an hour to make shoes and shirts and other goods that they will never have any hope of being able to afford themselves, sweatshops filled with women and children working in conditions that are often wantonly dangerous. One thing is simple—of course any person guided by natural reason, the norms of human decency, and the dictates of religion will desire for these poor workers to find their way into safer, better paying, and more fulfilling labor. But the complex question is how to effectively achieve that goal.

One strategy that many people latch onto is to boycott all such sweatshops. This strategy has several problems. The first is a knowledge problem. It's far from easy for Western consumers to accurately distinguish genuinely inhumane sweatshops from those factories that are actually relatively safe and providing their workers with substantially better pay than they could receive for other available work. We can no longer imagine living on wages that are only a tenth of what we make, but many people in the developing world regard such meager wages as a lavish salary increase sent down from heaven to lift their families out of extreme poverty. Boycott a factory like this and what have you accomplished?

You have wiped out a business that was boosting the incomes of many poor people and putting their families on the first rung of the ladder of economic progress; these are precisely the sort of factories in which many of our ancestors started their climb from extreme poverty on the multi-generational way to economic success.

So in addressing the problem of brutal sweatshops, the first task is not to impose the highly unusual economic standards of the developed world on regions that have only recently started up the ladder of economic development—lest we inadvertently stop that development in its tracks. Second, we must recognize that the force that has created many of the most brutal sweatshops isn't economic freedom but a mongrel cross of capitalism and government meddling—sometimes by the local governments, sometimes by neocolonial powers, usually by some devilish marriage of the two. Oftentimes people work in the hellish sweatshops because they lack the economic freedom to pursue better opportunities. If they possessed that freedom—if they weren't constantly bumping up against the unscalable wall of corporate-government cronyism masquerading as a free market—then these workers could pursue better opportunities. And if the sweatshop owners knew their workers could pursue better opportunities, the heartless employers would be forced to reform working conditions simply to retain competent workers.

This is what has occurred in Hong Kong. Jimmy Lai escaped from China to Hong Kong as a small boy. He got a job working long hours in a factory. He used that challenging opportunity to begin his climb out of poverty, and today he is a multi-millionaire. That's an extreme example, but the reality for the vast majority of people in Hong Kong today is not poverty but relative affluence—because the economy has been free to create new labor opportunities, and the laborers have been relatively free to pursue those opportunities, all within the context of a globalized island economy.

Globalization and Culture

Many of the ills of globalization are the result of top-down planning rather than free markets. But this realization needs to be balanced against another: global capitalism can't of itself supply the cultural and moral formation worthy of the human person and essential for human flourishing. Even if we could purge much of the cronyism and misguided central planning from the process of globalization, the global market wouldn't suddenly supply the cultural and moral formation essential for widespread economic and human flourishing. This is not the function of a market, as both the critics and supporters of an international process of globalization and free exchange need to understand clearly.

My friend the late Reverend Edmund Opitz put it this way: "The market will exhibit all the shortcomings and failures that people, in their peaceful acting, will exhibit."[1] What this means, among other things, is that our increasing interconnectedness holds great potential for offenses against human dignity. Advances in technology and communication can make it easier to sell pornography—or to traffic human beings. Or to give a less dire example, foreign investment allows for dispersed, non-localized ownership of businesses, which in turn can render their management less personal and less attuned to local customs and expectations.

Globalization also poses immense long-term challenges for culture. False and demeaning ideas can spread, sometimes more swiftly than truths that contribute to human flourishing. Because widespread skepticism now exists about universal and timeless truths, cultural freedom can be abused. The weak who seem to have little to offer—the poor, the unborn, the elderly, and the disabled—can be seen as a burden to be marginalized, limited, and even destroyed instead of being recognized as persons worthy of respect and solidarity.

Western mass media often does more harm than good when globalization extends its reach: the degradation of human sexuality, including the exploitation of women; the confusion between "having" and "being" (about which I will have more to say in Chapter Ten); and an inflated sense of our rights along with a lessening sense of social responsibility—these are just a few of the cultural manifestations of Western society that are worthy of critique and that can do real harm to the culture of a developing country once it gets plugged into the global information economy.

But these cultural problems are accompanied by positive opportunities, including an invitation for religious communities to do what it is they do best, which is to lead men and women to a conversion of life so that all their values and choices, including those in the economic sphere, reflect their encounter with the truth about God and human nature. One of the great resources that Christianity brings to the mission of ensuring that globalization serves the human person is its universality. Since "the Gospel is for all," as the old hymn says, and has been from the beginning, we are well situated to extend its message throughout the entire world. That truth and the community around it embolden us to proclaim unequivocally the absolute dignity of all human persons and to build political, charitable, and market institutions that reflect that dignity. The challenge now is to use the opportunities that globalization affords for a new evangelization that will transform the global culture for the better.

The idea that Christianity can and does play such a positive role isn't restricted to Christians or even theists. The English psychiatrist and social commentator Theodore Dalrymple, a professed atheist, has argued as much.[2] Former British MP and London *Times* columnist Matthew Parris made the same point in a December 2008 op-ed:

> Now a confirmed atheist, I've become convinced of the enormous contribution that Christian evangelism makes in Africa: sharply distinct from the work of secular NGOs, government projects and international aid efforts. These alone will not do. Education and training alone will not do. In Africa Christianity changes people's hearts. It brings a spiritual transformation. The rebirth is real. The change is good.[3]

There is a virtuous circle at work here. Christianity, a global religion, played a role in paving the way for economic globalization, and economic globalization then played a role in bringing more people into contact with other cultures and, with it, Christianity, which in turn brings more people into the fold of Christianity.

We shouldn't be distracted by the complexity of this historical process. Free trade is a process whereby the values that people hold are given expression in the form of goods and services which are demanded and supplied. To a significant extent, the culture and the values that determine what is bought and sold are already in place. The market does not create the culture or people's values so much as reveal them. Also, cultures are not static. When cultures encounter each other, a refining process can go on for reciprocal improvement. What this means is that the virtuous formation of a culture, which begins with the virtuous formation of people, is much more a moral enterprise than it is an economic one, and can only be effectively altered on that level.

What we find, then, is that the free market is neither the destructive boogeyman that its detractors on the left make it out to be nor an elixir that can bless a society absent a moral context. Capitalism has the power to create even as it replaces older forms of creating and serving, and with a strength and energy unknown to centrally planned economies, but only if it is a system of enterprise governed by the rule of law and a respect for the dignity and capacity of the human person—only, in other words, if it is a just capitalism.

Suggestions for Further Reading

James D. Gwartney, Richard L. Stroup, Dwight R. Lee, and Tawni H. Ferrarini, *Common Sense Economics: What Everyone Should Know About Wealth and Prosperity* (St. Martin's Press, 2010).

John R. Lott Jr., *Freedomnomics: Why the Free Market Works and Other Half-Baked Theories Don't* (Regnery, 2007).

Stephen Moore and Julian L. Simon, *It's Getting Better All the Time: 100 Greatest Trends of the Last 100 Years* (Cato Institute, 2000).

Johan Norberg, *In Defense of Global Capitalism* (Cato Institute, 2003).

Joseph A. Schumpeter, *Capitalism, Socialism, and Democracy* (Harper and Brothers, 1942).

Rev. Robert A. Sirico, ed., *Globalization, Economics, and the Family* (Libereria Editrice Vaticana, 2002).

CHAPTER 5

Why Greed Is *Not* Good—and Why You Can Get More of It with Socialism than with Capitalism

Q: Maybe socialism doesn't work, but at least it's idealistic. Capitalism may be the system that produces the most material wealth. But doesn't *laissez-faire* mean capitulating to people's baser instincts—just giving in to the notion that people are really motivated by nothing nobler than greed?

■ ■ ■

A: Greed is not good. But capitalism doesn't require greed. A successful entrepreneur can be motivated by things other than greed. What capitalism can do far more effectively than socialism is prod a person's greedy impulses toward socially useful ends. Under socialism, greed's primary outlet is exploitation—legal or illegal. The greedy man under socialism can't get rich by starting and nurturing a socially useful business. All he can do is become a thief or a cream-skimming government insider. Under capitalism, he has another option: he can excel in a socially useful business. In this way, capitalism provides the greedy person a socially beneficent alternative to exploitation.

■ ■ ■

Remember villainous business executive Gordon Gekko in Oliver Stone's 1987 film *Wall Street*? "Greed is good," he claimed. Unfortunately, many real-life defenders of capitalism argue along the same lines. Greed, they claim, is the stimulant that drives the economy. And critics of the free market readily agree—they hate capitalism because they believe it fosters greed.

I say a plague on both their houses. Greed isn't good, and it isn't the essence of capitalism. Greed is not necessary to the process of wealth creation in a capitalist economy. Greed exists in every capitalist economy, of course—because you find greed everywhere there are human beings. But if you want to discover the optimal breeding ground for the vice of greed (and envy, greed's twin), look not to the free market, but to socialism in its various incarnations.

As for capitalism, it isn't based on greed; it isn't fueled and fired by greed. It is fueled by human creativity in a system that rewards people for serving the wants and needs of others. For the successful entrepreneur, greed is optional.

To understand why, we need to move below the surface of the market to explore the real motivations of buyers and sellers. We also need to take a look at the moral dimension of central planning and forced redistribution.

What Is Greed?

Let's start by distinguishing what greed is from what it isn't. Having a clear understanding of the vice can help us avoid falsely accusing others of greed—and also help us better resist the vice in our own lives.

When critics describe capitalism as "greedy," they may mean any number of things. Embedded in the word is a cluster of interrelated vices: envy, pride, covetousness, materialism, cowardice, miserliness, and consumerism. It is impossible to delineate here all the distinctions among these concepts, so let's try to get to the heart of the matter. All these vices are related in various ways to the Latin *avere*, literally "to crave," from which we get the English word avarice. Of course, mere craving or desire is not wrong. If you haven't eaten today it is quite natural for you to crave a meal; in fact, it is morally incumbent upon you to eat at some point, lest you starve to death. What turns a normal desire into a vice is when the craving becomes unbalanced, when it becomes a kind of addiction or idol, what a theologian would call "inordinate"—unbalanced or unreasonable. Avarice is the unreasonable desire for what we do not have and the determination to obtain it without regard to others.

We need to keep in mind that the vice of avarice does not apply only to material things. Greed can be an unbalanced interest in riches for their own sake, but it can also develop out of a person's desire for status, prestige, or even another person. Avoiding this particular moral failing is all about maintaining balance in our relation to the world.

Greed is known as one of the seven capital sins because greedy people will go to great lengths to obtain their object, committing other sins on the way to getting what they want—even to the point of using fellow human beings as instruments, as though they were not creatures with intrinsic value and dignity, ends in and of themselves rather than the mere means to another person's wishes.

The opposite of the greed-is-good error is the notion that desire of any kind is wrong. But the capacity to desire is actually a good thing that's built in to the human condition. To desire to live better than our ancestors, to give our children a better life than we have had, to be more comfortable ourselves than in the past—these are not immoral things. They become morally problematic when material betterment becomes the whole end and focus of our lives, trumping the more important moral and spiritual goods.

It's undeniable that there are many businesspeople afflicted with an unbalanced obsession with material betterment, but it's important to recognize that the sin of greed is without professional boundaries. Even those professions often characterized as community-minded or altruistic have their share of practitioners who are nonetheless driven by avarice:

in politics, in social work, in public service, in health care and, yes, in the church. (The great Renaissance writer Dante Alighieri was so disgusted by ambitious clergy that, in his classic *Inferno*, he consigned a large number of them to hell!) In sum, the identification of greed with profit and generosity with not-for-profit is too simplistic. As tempting as it may be, we cannot demonize profit and canonize poverty.

The Role of Profits

Profits are central to capitalism, and I am often asked whether profit-making is evidence of greed. Not in itself. The fact that a business is profitable tells us little that is morally relevant. Profit, after all, is simply the name that accounting attaches to the condition of income outpacing costs.[1] In other words, a company that earns a profit brings in more money than it expends for all of it costs, including materials, real estate, labor, and taxes. The opposite of profits is financial loss. And a firm that is losing rather than making money cannot long survive. So, under ordinary circumstances, profits are a necessary condition for the success and continuation of a business.

Of course the government can bail out unprofitable businesses at taxpayers' expense. But that only shifts the need for profits to the other—profitable—enterprises that pay the taxes. Bail out enough unprofitable people and companies, and the profitable ones start wondering why they are working so hard. When a company is not profitable, it is a sign that something is wrong with the firm: maybe its manufacturing methods are inefficient, its overhead is excessive, its products are in need of revamping, or any number of other possible weaknesses. Government support simply suppresses the incentive to improve, delaying reforms that are necessary to bring the company back to economic health. History is littered with examples of dysfunctional companies bailed out by government: a double blow to the consuming public, which is deprived of both the benefits that an improved company would bring to the market as well as a large amount of its tax money spent to shore up the dysfunctional company's finances.[2]

Profitable companies are the ones that find a way to create and deliver products and services at prices high enough to cover their costs, but low enough that customers find them attractive. The profitable company, in other words, is one that flourishes by creating and delivering value.

This positive dimension of business is often obscured by the common stereotype of the greedy capitalist—a stereotype epitomized in the images on the Chance and Community Chest cards in the board game Monopoly: a well-fed businessman in a top hat smoking a cigar. He simultaneously represents big business and the successful Monopoly player who is growing rich through luck and cutthroat competition. Victory in Monopoly comes not when a player gets rich by creating new value in a business enterprise but instead when a player has successfully taken everyone else's money and driven them all into bankruptcy. Monopoly, then, is literally a zero-sum *game*. But it seems that some people confuse the real world with a game of Monopoly—and fall into the fallacy of thinking that people can gain in a marketplace only if others lose. For instance, if there are poor people, clearly it must be because the rich have taken such a massive piece of some pre-existing pie that there was hardly any left over for the poor folks. If that's the case, the obvious solution is to forcibly divide up the pie in a more equitable way.

But perhaps the pie wasn't always just sitting there, the exact same size from all eternity. Maybe many of the rich didn't take more than their fair share; maybe they *made* more than their fair share. The zero-sum assumption prevents people from ever asking whether the solution to poverty might be to grow the pie even more.

This zero-sum mentality is particularly prevalent among clergy, who often view profits with disdain. In conversations with fellow clergy who take this view, I often ask, if profits are morally dubious, are losses more ethical? The point is to shed light on the nature of profit and loss. Both are tools for understanding a company's health. Profits indicate that resources are being used wisely by a business; losses suggest that they are not. Although profits and losses are not the be-all and end-all of a company, they are crucial first-level indicators of how effectively they are serving the wants or needs of customers.

Because human wants always outpace scarce resources, every society must have some guide for allocating those resources. Something or someone must decide whether water will be used for drinking, bathing, or irrigation, and whether iron ore will be used for making cars or manufacturing tractors. The same is true for all social resources. Even the resource of time, which is also scarce, requires some tool for sensible allocation.

One solution to the problem of allocating scarce resources is to control marketplace decisions and resources from some central point. To varying degrees, this is the strategy advocated by socialism in its different forms. As we have learned from bitter experience, the problem with this strategy for allocating resources is that it concentrates enormous power in a few hands. And excessive power tends to do nasty things to human nature. But there's also a second problem—the knowledge problem. Even if the political elite controlling the economy were morally perfect, they still wouldn't have enough information to effectively allocate all of the human and material resources effectively. These twin problems have hampered or undone every centrally planned economy in history.

Fortunately, there is an alternative strategy for allocating scare resources: the network of prices that arises naturally from voluntary exchanges among buyers and sellers in a marketplace. Here the laws of economics come into play. A lower price for any particular good signals relative abundance; people can buy more of that good. A higher price signals relative scarcity, forcing people to economize their use of the good. Through this system, where the prices of goods and services are constantly in flux, consumers can balance their needs against the availability of various goods and know at any moment how much of each they should purchase and use, and producers can know how much of a good they should produce and sell. Prices help us determine whether a good or service is being wasted and therefore should not be in production, or if it is highly desired and therefore more of it should be produced. For instance, when entrepreneurs discovered how to pump, store, refine, and use petroleum oil, its price dropped well below that of whale oil. Whale oil was priced out of the market, and there was less pressure to kill whales for their fat.

Profit can also be understood as a kind of price signal. Making a profit indicates to a company that it is performing its tasks in a way that a segment of the public approves—not just notionally, in opinions they might give a pollster, but with their hard-earned cash. Losses inform the managers and owners that they need to make adjustments or turn to other pursuits so that social resources are not wasted. Thus the signaling device of profit and loss serves an irreplaceable economic function. Profitability serves as a motivating force, but also—and more importantly—it signifies a job well done.

An important caveat: the social obligations of the business do not stop with profitably delivering goods and services. Business must deal honestly, keep their contracts, serve the community in the broadest sense, and be attentive to the moral dimensions of the investment process. The price system does not magically guarantee moral behavior. To give a painful but all too realistic example, the price system in a depraved society may signal that the most valued use of young women from poor families is for them to become prostitutes. Confusion arises when people see such evils and mistakenly assume that getting rid of the free market will somehow magically solve the problem. Only a little reflection should reveal the error. Moving to a command-and-control economy doesn't remove lust and selfishness from the human heart. Those vices go right on thriving. Only now they are fed and cared for by some arm of the state—with the added problem that poor families have even fewer alternative economic options because the command-and-control economy has placed a host of morally preferable enterprises beyond their reach. While the price system in a free economy does not provide a moral foundation for a society, and while it doesn't remove opportunities for ill-gotten gain, it handily beats every form of socialism at providing moral and socially beneficent options for escaping poverty.

Excess Profits?

Those who accept the role of profits may nonetheless complain about the existence of "excess profits." But what constitutes an excess profit? Did Thomas Edison garner "excess profit" from his lucrative invention of the light bulb, an invention that has by now enriched the lives of billions of people? On the other hand, what about a company that turned only a modest 3 percent profit last year, but did so by deceiving its customers?

The charge of inordinate profit-making is usually lodged against particular businesses or industries for reasons that have little to do with objective accounting and a lot to do with aesthetic distaste, personal dislike, ideological disapproval, or some similar factor. For example, every time gas prices climb there are rumblings about "big oil" taking "excessive profits." Many don't think to ask whether there might be good economic reasons for such price adjustments. Instead they assume that rapidly rising prices must mean oil companies are gouging consumers. In fact, while oil company profits rise and fall depending on various market factors, on the whole, they are well in line with the profits of firms in other industries. For the first quarter of 2011—a time when oil executives were under fire from political grandstanders—the profit margin for the big oil company sector averaged 6.1 cents per dollar of revenue, ranking it 114th out of 215 industries.[3] Where was the outcry over excessive profits in software, publishing, railroads, or any of the dozens of other business sectors that were more lucrative than the big oil companies?

Even extraordinary profit margins serve a necessary function. High profits signal to other entrepreneurs that the public is demanding more of a particular good or service than is being produced. When businessmen notice the high profits of others, new investors and creators enter the market to meet the demand. Notice also that the competitive bidding for resources and public attention means no company is in an automatically profitable position. A business can only continually earn high profits through a combination of hard work, creativity, and vision that allows it to deliver value far more efficiently or richly than any of its competitors. This market dynamic spurs more effective modes of production, since companies are constantly looking for new and creative ways to deliver value more richly or efficiently than their competitors.

Where outsized profits persist over a long period of time, this is often a symptom not of capitalism but of the lack of market freedom. If new producers are not entering a field that is providing big profits, it is often because government is restricting competition. The answer is to get the government out of the business of picking winners and losers in the marketplace. The solution, in other words, is to move away from command-and-control cronyism and toward freer and more transparent capitalism.

Moral Profits

The benefits of the price system are innumerable. Consumers rely on prices every day to make decisions. The price system allows businessmen to think far into the future. It allows the public to partake in the ownership of companies through an active market for capital, and to try their hand at entrepreneurship. It grants to everybody the incentive to work and better themselves by cultivating the material world as responsible stewards.

A pastor may call on a businessman to give up his profits for the sake of his soul. Whether that is prudent pastoral advice depends on the individual's circumstances. Jesus called on the rich young man to sell everything he had and to follow Jesus in his ministry. We can only surmise that he saw into the man's heart and recognized a need for extreme measures. (It is interesting to note, however, that Jesus commanded him to *sell* his belongings and then give to the poor, conferring a greater benefit than if he had just given his belongings directly to them.) What we do know is that the Gospels record various other instances of Jesus interacting with wealthy people, and in none of the other cases does he tell them to sell everything they have and give it to the poor. The case of the rich young man seems to be a lot less about the economic status of the young man than about the Christian moral life as a call to go beyond the bare minimum contained in the negative commandments of the Decalogue; it is about heroism, not economics. All disciples of Christ are called to lives of generosity and detachment even from the things we do possess, as we strive to be good stewards of the material resources within our care.

The sixteenth-century priest, Francis de Sales, when called upon to give pastoral advice to Christians involved in trades and occupations, gave a different answer from what some might expect from a saint: "Have greater care than worldly men do to make your property profitable and fruitful . . . our possessions are not our own. God has given them to us to cultivate and he wants us to make them fruitful and profitable . . . therefore let us exercise this gracious care of preserving and even of increasing our temporal goods whenever just occasions present themselves."[4]

The system of profit and loss in a free economy can orient our behavioral compass toward activities that serve others, make good use of resources, and prepare us for the future. It doesn't block people from serving evil desires, but without the price signals in a free economy, our economic activities would be without order.

It is a helpful thought experiment to imagine how long moral behavior and social order would last in a world without any prices—and hence without the ability to calculate profit and loss. Stripped of the ability to assess the value and availability of various goods and services, such a society would quickly devolve into confusion and chaos. A crucial form of guidance, one that helps us manage our innumerable daily economic activities, would be stripped away, the division of labor would crumble, and the standard of living would be systematically reduced until we reached a primitive stage. A world without monetary calculation would be a world in disarray.

Beyond Gordon Gekko

Another way to reflect on the morality of business enterprise is to look at those who are economically successful and attempt to discern their motivation. The Michelin Company is an international corporation with successful brands in products such as tires, heavy machinery, and travel and dining guides. Francois Michelin, the wealthy patriarch of this dynasty, is in many people's minds virtually synonymous with globalized industrial capitalism. So when people find out that I have known the man for many years, I am often asked what he is like. One encounter, I think, captures the Francois Michelin I know.

In the spring of 2000 I was travelling in Europe and Mr. Michelin asked if I would stop off at his home town of Clermont Ferrand in central France and visit the world headquarters of the Michelin Company. As I alighted from the plane, I was on the lookout for a driver holding a placard with my name on it—thinking I would be chauffeured to the company's offices. Instead, once I retrieved my bags, I was greeted by the modest Michelin in his usual simple grey suit. The seventy-seven-year-old tycoon (clearly recognized by people in the airport) reached to assist me with my suitcases. I initially declined, but after some insistence on his part, I handed him one of the lighter bags, and we walked to the parking lot, where he approached a nondescript automobile and opened the trunk. As I circled around to the passenger seat, I glanced down to see if the tires were Michelin. I did not see the signature brand markings. Once seated in the car I joked with Mr. Michelin, "I see that you are not driving on Michelin tires."

"Mon Père [as he usually addresses me], let me show you something."

He pointed to a contraption that sat between the two of us in the front seat of the car. It looked something like a taxicab meter. He began to press various buttons on the device and as he did so, the readout changed each time, jumping from the front right to the front left location, then to the back right and the back left locations. Each time different numbers would appear.

"You are correct to observe these are not Michelin tires—not yet. This is a test car, and this meter lets me know the relative stress and heat on each of the experimental tires."

"You mean you are not yet sure these tires are secure?" I asked.

"I hope you will not worry. Our scientists have worked hard on these tires. But you would not expect me to offer tires for sale to my customers to drive their families on, if I were not willing to ride on them first."

At the time, the headlines in the newspapers were filled with details of the controversy surrounding reports of Firestone tires on certain Ford vehicles failing. The controversy would eventually end the hundred-year-old relationship between the two companies. In light of this, I asked Michelin if his business was good.

He replied with a frown, "It is a terrible moment for those of us in the tire business, terrible."

This was an unexpected answer, since I thought his business would have benefited from Firestone's loss of prestige. But Mr. Michelin's instinctual reply was to lament the crisis. He said that any time an industry fails in protecting its customers it injures trust in the whole industry—a negative outcome for everyone involved.

This snapshot of Francois Michelin does not, of course, disprove the existence of unprincipled Gordon Gekkos in the world of high finance and enterprise. But there is nothing in business or the market economy that mandates a selfish dog-eat-dog ethic.

The Apostle of Selfishness

We began this chapter with Gordon Gekko announcing that greed is good. As he goes on to say to the shareholders of the fictional Teldar Paper Corporation, "Greed clarifies, cuts through, and captures the essence of the evolutionary spirit. Greed, in all of its forms—greed for life, for money, for love, knowledge—has marked the upward surge of mankind. And greed—you mark my words—will not only save Teldar Paper, but that other malfunctioning corporation called the U.S.A."

Some would argue that the roots of this way of thinking reach decades back to the teachings of the Russian-born novelist and philosopher Ayn Rand, considered by many to be the Apostle of Greed for her defense of capitalism. The reality is a bit more complicated. Rand did not actually defend "greed." Rather, she defended a notion of "radical individualism" or "rational self-interest," which she describes in her provocatively entitled book, *The Virtue of Selfishness.*

Rand tended to play with language and employ words in idiosyncratic ways. She condemned altruism, sacrifice, and self-sacrifice ("the surrender of a greater value for the sake of a lesser one or of a non-value")[5] but what she meant by those terms is not what most people mean. The conventional meaning of the word selfishness is not "concern with one's own interest" (one of the dictionary definitions Rand selected to base her definition on in the introduction to her book). Most people understand being "selfish" more along the lines of what ones finds in Merriam-Webster, "concerned excessively or exclusively with oneself: seeking or concentrating on one's own advantage, pleasure, or well-being without regard for others."

Is her idiosyncratic use of language evidence of rhetorical daring or simply of muddled thinking? I have no desire to engage in a treatise on language and rhetoric here, and I suspect you have little interest in reading one; but I do think, given Rand's impact on many contemporary defenders of economic liberty, we would do well to examine a critical flaw in her anthropology.

Rand's idea of man is noble, and she is second to no one in defending his freedom in the face of the totalitarian impulse, which she saw firsthand as she grew up in the newly formed Soviet Union. She wrote passionately about man's creative capacity and entrepreneurial potential, and about the need for social conditions that protect man's freedom to be creative rather than crush him under the collective and collectivist weight of regulation, taxes, and the disdain for individual human rights that inevitably accompanies grand socialist plans.

These themes can be riveting and inspiring in Ayn Rand's novels, but her foundational belief in radical individualism—an autonomy that precludes social obligation and responsibility—is problematic. In fact the selfishness and radical individualism at the heart of Rand's defense of capitalism stand in conflict with the very institutions that Rand wants to defend. The free market system rests on the fact that human beings are not just individual but also social beings. Contracts, communities, markets, language, trade, exchange—all of these forms of social engagement are hallmarks of the market economy.

When some of my European friends try to envision a capitalism that would temper the individualism they complain about in the free economy, they speak of a "social market." But the phrase is a redundancy. What market is not social? After all, the entrepreneur in a free market—far more than the government bureaucrat or central planner under socialism—must submit himself to the wants and needs of the consumer if he is to profit. Entrepreneurs cannot even unilaterally determine the price of the goods they put on the market—not if they want to move their products and stay in business. Instead, the prices and types of products in the market are guided by the wants and needs of consumers, whose purchases reflect their priorities and values.

The labor market is similarly social. If a society has extended economic freedom to all of its citizens, then business owners will be competing with a host of other enterprises and opportunities in their efforts to attract and retain employees. The entrepreneur and future employee voluntarily arrive at a mutually agreeable arrangement, and the result is that social bond known as the employer-employee relationship. Of course many markets are far from economically free—a state of affairs that leads to everything from persistently outsized profit margins enjoyed by government-protected monopolies to a glut of artificially cheap labor as the poor are blocked from pursuing a host of possible enterprises and so are left at the mercy of large employers. In such cases a low-paying factory job may represent the best and brightest opportunity the poor have, so the solution isn't to shut down the factories. The solution is to push for greater economic freedom for the poor, so that they can become consumers of job opportunities among a smorgasbord of choices, as you find in a free and developed economy.

A free labor market encourages employers to behave more sociably toward their employees—to treat them better—since they know that their workers have other opportunities. At the same time the workers in a free economy know that excellence is rewarded by employers who are competing for the best workers—so that workers are encouraged to serve their employers with energy and purpose.

The Socialist Mirage

All of this is the opposite of what existed under Soviet socialism. That tragic experiment made clear that the various forms of central planning, the major alternative to the capitalist organization of an economy, severely undermine the social cooperation that the market promotes.

From its beginning advocates of socialism have touted its benefits in humanitarian terms. Karl Marx himself, in *The Communist Manifesto*, advocated violent revolution only as a precursor to a harmonious society. "In place of the old bourgeois society, with its classes and class antagonisms, we shall have an association, in which the free development of each is the condition for the free development of all."[6]

It didn't quite turn out that way.

Where a socialist organization of economic life has held sway, the result has not been the rise of social cooperation but its opposite—the decline of civil society and an increase in alienation.

This phenomenon was on display in the Soviet Union and its East European bloc, where fascinating and disturbing information concerning life under the totalitarian state has gradually come to light over the two decades since communism fell. The elimination of the profit motive did not diminish selfishness; it removed the brakes on selfishness that a capitalist system provides. Without incentives to care about whether their customers were satisfied, store clerks and managers of state-run enterprises were notoriously indifferent to the needs of consumers.

In a free economy, greed isn't necessary to the functioning of the market but, at the same time, a greedy person has all manner of socially beneficial ways to try to sate his avarice. Any legal and wholesome good or service that he can provide more efficiently or richly than his competitors—whether it be the services of a skilled heart surgeon, the services of a well run cleaning company, or the low prices of an efficiently run roofing business—can allow a greedy person to obtain wealth while serving society at large. You don't have to be greedy to succeed in any of these pursuits. You may want to pursue excellence and provide a living for yourself and your family. Other people may be greedy. But in a free market economy the most efficient way for those people to pursue their disproportionate love of wealth is generally to subordinate themselves to the service of others. They cannot satisfy their greed without helping other people.

In the opposite sort of economy, such as existed in the Soviet Union, the primary way the greedy person pursued riches was either to enter a black market of vice or to work his way up in the Communist Party, which amounted to organized criminal brutality and exploitation on a national scale.

The material deprivation that communist economies produced did not lead to generosity and detachment from material possessions. Instead, acquiring the basic material goods needed for sustenance became the all-consuming preoccupation of those not fortunate enough to occupy important positions in the Party. People tended to look at each other as a means of access to scarce items. Dishonesty and cynicism reigned supreme. "We pretend to work and you pretend to pay us," was the common joke.[7]

In sum, materialism—that central charge that many moral critics make against capitalism—was worse under socialist regimes than it ever was in a market economy. The domination of materialism under socialism had devastating consequences on the spiritual lives of those trapped within its boundaries. If we really care about cultivating the traits of generosity and concern for others, we should promote positive culture-forming institutions within a free society—not chase after a utopian ideal that ends in the suppression of the impulses that make us human.

The Personable Person and the Market

I hope by now it's clear that the answer to radical individualism is not socialist collectivism, but also that the answer to socialist collectivism is not radical individualism. The human person from the first moment of existence is simultaneously social and individual, autonomous and at the same time in relationship. Human beings start out as biologically distinct organisms, but in intimate relationship with their mothers. This fundamental pattern extends throughout the person's life, for the human person is by nature an autonomous creature in relationship with both other persons and other things. We gain a certain amount of independence as we grow, but we still stay in relationship, either with our families or with others. Language itself is an aspect of both our individual and our social nature. Human beings are not strictly autonomous entities; we are built for social interaction and relationships.

Building a society in which we can be fulfilled first requires an understanding of who we are. If we get the anthropology—the science of the human person—wrong, we get the whole thing wrong. Seeing human beings as mere individuals attenuates our rich complexity just as much as seeing us as mere cogs in some collectivist historical dialectic does. We are autonomous beings, but we came from someone. We are the result of a communion of love. We reach outside of ourselves for love and knowledge. Children result from and expand this social aspect of our nature. And we even have a destiny for communion outside this world. To attempt to build a society on a foundation of radical individualism, which ignores the reality of human solidarity and society itself, would be to construct a ruthless, cold, libertine environment unworthy of human persons. And in any case, such a society—which is radically opposed to a truly free society—would not long endure.

The best entrepreneurs are those who have a highly fine-tuned sense of the desires—and potential desires—of ordinary people. This is a rare ability; otherwise it would be easy to be a successful entrepreneur. That isn't to say that this capacity is without moral pitfalls. People's desires are not always good, helpful, or healthy, either from a moral or a physical point of view. So the talent of determining what consumers want is not itself virtuous, when detached from moral concerns. It is useful, but not always good. It can satisfy base lusts or noble yearnings. That is why it is so important that actors in the economy be formed in sound habits that promote human flourishing rather than human degradation.

So it is possible for entrepreneurs to promote corrupting goods and services—internet pornography, to give one highly lucrative example. But it is also possible for them to serve their fellow human beings with goods and services that make our lives better.

Not that you'd know this from the media. Whether it's books, movies, or television (or board games), you rarely find a positive portrayal of business. Even when the media try to celebrate entrepreneurship, it comes across as morally meaningless—I give you *The Apprentice.* Was there any sense of nobility presented in that series? A lot of creativity, and a lot of longing for jets and helicopters and lovely resorts, but what about the discipline and the loyalty, the courage and commitment to excellence, the striving to understand and empathize with the wants and needs of the customer—the whole cluster of virtues, I can say without hesitation, that describes the vast majority of successful entrepreneurs I have come to know personally in my work? These people are not saints. I am describing people whose very virtues and talents have left them vulnerable to all of the temptations of status and success. But they have succeeded only by exercising real virtues—virtues that have more than a taste of human nobility about them. Where were such men and women on *The Apprentice*? I looked for them in vain.

Suggestions for Further Reading

Pope John Paul II, *Centesimus Annus*, May 1991, available online at http://www.vatican.va/holy_father/john_paul_ii/encyclicals/documents/hf_jp-ii_enc_01051991_centesimus-annus_en.html.

Robert G. Kennedy, *The Good That Business Does* (Acton Institute, 2006).

F. A. Hayek, *The Fatal Conceit: The Errors of Socialism* (University of Chicago, 1991).

Jay Richards, *Money, Greed, and God: Why Capitalism is the Solution and Not the Problem* (HarperOne, 2010).

Ludwig von Mises, *Socialism: An Economic and Sociological Analysis* (Yale University Press, 1951 [1922]).

CHAPTER 6

The Idol of Equality

Q: Aren't we all supposed to be equal? And yet the gap between rich and poor just keeps growing. We need to maintain equality among people. Isn't vigorous government action necessary to keep the playing field level—to keep the wealthy and powerful from taking more than their fair share and running roughshod over everyone else?

■ ■ ■

A: All people are inherently equal in their rights and dignity. But the attempt to create perfect equality in everything (which is really the pursuit of sameness) is bound to fail. And worse than fail: whenever and wherever absolute equality has been pursued, terrible consequences have followed. The challenge is for society to bring people's diverse talents into harmonious cooperation in exchanges that benefit everyone involved—not vainly attempt to impose a straitjacket sameness on everyone.

■ ■ ■

Having paid a few brief visits to several of the Occupy Wall Street locations around the U.S., it is now clear to me that the leftist idealism of a previous generation has not dissipated some forty years later. The sights and sounds—and even some of the smells (sadly, I jest not)—are all too familiar. Even the name of the movement isn't new, though many may be hearing it for the first time. Student demonstrators at Columbia or Berkeley in the 1960s would "occupy" a campus building so as to disrupt the normal course of business. "To occupy," tellingly, suggests seizing and maintaining control over a space as if by conquest. There is no hint in this verb of any intention to create anything, to build anything. The "occupy" meme has its roots in the fixed-pie fallacy. If there's only one pie and it's always going to be the same size, then the only way for the 99 percent ever to possess some of what the 1 percent have is for them to seize it.

In another bit of nostalgia, I noted that the Occupiers at one of the sites I visited had a sign which I have seen from time to time at similar gatherings. It read, "Eat the Rich." If it is possible to encapsulate an entire social philosophy into three words, that sign may have accomplished it. Let's unpack it.

The Value of the 1 Percent

The Occupy crowd views the rich, the 1 percent, as exploiters. As I say, this, again, is the old zero-sum-game fallacy. If someone has an abundance, he must have acquired it at the expense of someone else. The proof is in the fact that the Occupiers make little or no effort to distinguish between, say, a multi-millionaire who grew rich from serving the 99 percent conscientiously and effectively versus some corrupt insider who got ahead by swindling someone or cutting sweetheart deals with government insiders. Not "Eat the Dishonest Rich," or "Eat the Corrupt Insiders." No, just eat everyone with a net worth over some arbitrary amount.

When as a '70s socialist I first began exploring the idea that the free economy could be based on a solid moral foundation, I asked what seemed to me to be an obvious question, and one that I still believe is legitimate: Aren't the rich getting richer and the poor getting poorer? With wealth being ever more unevenly distributed, doesn't it make sense for the poor to "eat the rich"—not literally, but in the sense of an aggressive and wholesale redistribution of wealth from rich to poor?

Like many progressives, I was concerned that the rich owned a disproportionate amount. Today, the differences are as eye-catching as ever. This country's 1 percent owns upwards of 40 percent of the wealth. That's 40 percent of the wealth of the richest country in the world. This simple math struck me as overwhelming: Some people obviously have too little. Surely redistributing the treasure trove that the 1 percent were sitting on was the obvious solution to their poverty.

The redistribution solution was actually less of a "slam dunk" than I realized. Let's do another thought experiment, assuming for a moment that we could redistribute the wealth of the rich without destroying the economy. Let's do the experiment on the global scale, since the most dramatic instances of economic inequality exist between the rich in the developed world and those in extreme poverty in developing countries. What does the math tell us? If we confiscated all of the wealth of the world's richest 1 percent—every last penny—we could distribute about $13,000 to every person on the planet—one time.[1] In the absence of marketable skills and billions of new job opportunities, how much good would that one-time $13,000 windfall do for the average poor person in the long term?

But that kind of redistribution would actually be worse than ineffective. What I failed to see as a Left Coast socialist is that the vast majority of the wealth of the 1 percent isn't simply being sat on by the rich. What finally alerted me to my error in reasoning was my friend's answer when I related to him my dream of solving poverty by redistributing wealth. I had pointed him to the math and suggested that common decency demanded an immediate and aggressive redistribution of all of this wealth. But imagine, he responded, that we did what you want to do, that we redistribute all the wealth of the 1 percent to the poor so that there is greater equality of possession. What would happen then?

Almost everyone would be better off, I replied. Certainly the very wealthy would be poorer than before the redistribution, but the living standards of the poor would be raised dramatically.

"Are you sure?" he asked. "If your end goal is simply to even things out for a brief moment in time, then your proposal makes sense. But if your aim is to leave people better off over the long term, that's another matter. Think about it. Where would people work once all the wealth of the richest 1 percent was redistributed?"

That pulled me up full stop—for the simple reason that I never had actually stopped to think about it.

When most people picture the 1 percent and their wealth, what comes to mind is designer clothing and jewelry, yachts and limousines, mansions and penthouses—all sorts of alluring and attention-grabbing luxuries. Luxuries so distracting, in fact, that we tend to lose sight of the fact that most of the wealth of the wealthiest is invested. It is put to work in the businesses they own and manage, and in stocks and other financial vehicles that provide the capital for countless other businesses. These are the businesses that provide the 99 percent with the goods, services, and employment that they regularly enjoy and often take for granted.

Whether it's a big automotive plant or a small bakery on the corner, a microchip manufacturer or a family farm, all businesses that produce goods and employ people are owned by someone. It's businesses that make up most of the wealth of the 1 percent. Confiscating that wealth and giving it to the other 99 percent would mean shifting much of that wealth from investment and production to consumption, since the poor and middle class consume a far higher percentage of their income than the wealthy do. This sudden shift from investment and production to consumption would demolish the infrastructure that makes jobs, goods, and services possible.

We hear a great deal of angst expressed about the gap between the rich and the poor. But how morally significant is it that Bill Gates has tens of billions more than, say, my doctor, who lives in a very nice house—but with only one kitchen, while Gates has six? Is such a gap really a moral outrage? The second highest quintile of American households make about $60,000 a year on average, while the third highest live on $40,000. Is that an outrage? The smallest income gaps are actually in some of the poorest countries in the world, where the quantitative gap between the richest and the poorest is far smaller than it is between a middle class American and Bill Gates. Those societies are more equal, and yet people there are dying from dirty drinking water, malnutrition, and preventable diseases. This should tell us something. For one thing, it's impossible to measure real inequality in dollar amounts.

Measured that way, the gap in income between my doctor and Bill Gates is much bigger than the gap between two people in a developing country, one who has access to clean drinking water and one who doesn't—but the second, smaller gap is much more likely to mean the difference between health and sickness, maybe even life and death. The real moral problem is not that a few people like Bill Gates are enormously wealthier than the rest of us. The real moral problem is that some people lack the basic necessities of life, along with the opportunity to earn those basic necessities in a free society.

Mind the Floor, Not the Ceiling

Sometimes one hears calls for a "cap" or a ceiling on income. In 1942 President Franklin D. Roosevelt proposed to Congress that incomes for Americans be limited to $25,000 a year—about $350,000 in today's dollars. Although Roosevelt's proposal did not become law, Congress did levy a 90 percent income tax on Americans making more than $25,000.

But caps on income are counterproductive, if what we want is more for the poor. Let's look at an example from the private sector. From its inception in 1978, Ben & Jerry's Ice Cream has been a "progressive" business, supporting a variety of causes popular on the left. It was founded by two life-long friends, Ben Cohen and Jerry Greenfield, whose policy was never to permit anyone working for the company to earn more than seven times the amount of its entry-level employees—until, that is, Ben and Jerry's well-intentioned policy met the reality of the open market.

When they decided to sell the company and began the search for a new CEO who, they announced, would make only marginally more than the rest of the workers at the company, they discovered that no one with the requisite skills to run what by now had become a large corporation would apply for the position.[2]

Think about why this is so. It is not because others did not support the social aims of Ben and Jerry. It is not even because no one applied for the position. It is just that people with the requisite skills and experience to keep Ben & Jerry's in operation were too valuable to the market to work under the ceiling set by the company's founders.

Eventually, Ben and Jerry simply sold the company to the Unilever conglomerate, which ended the seven-to-one policy.

Differences in remuneration are important signals to the market. More highly paid professions entice more people to enter, despite the formidable challenges of extended education, long working hours, or stressful conditions. Lower pay sends a message that there is a surplus of available workers; thus if you seek a higher wage you should acquire additional training, move to another region, or take on a more strenuous job. In a properly functioning market there is nothing morally wrong with income differences *per se*.

The real moral problem is not the gap in wages between the lowest- and highest-paid workers, which is what a wage ceiling addresses. The real moral question is about the floor—how the poorest and most marginal people in any given society are doing. America's Catholic bishops acknowledged as much in their 1986 pastoral letter on the economy, *Economic Justice for All*, a relatively "center-left"-leaning document: as they put it, "The impact of national economic policies on the poor and the vulnerable is the primary criterion for judging their moral value."[3]

When you think about it, the rage for income equality is rather curious in the contemporary social climate. "Diversity" is celebrated (even obsessed over) and individuality praised, yet so many are looking to equality as a prescription for human flourishing. All of people's varied talents, interests, and backgrounds—all of the rich diversity that makes human beings so interesting—renders egalitarian utopianism unworkable.

Do We Know Who We Are?

Still, in a profound sense, human beings *are* equal. An anecdote nicely illustrates this fact. I especially like this story because my work involves spending a lot of time in airports.

A weather delay grounded all of the planes at a major U.S. airport. A businessman—apparently a real Type A sort—went to the airline representative and asked if he could get onto a flight out. She explained once again that the situation was due to conditions beyond her control. He insisted that he had an important meeting, that he was an important man, that he was flying first class, and that surely there was something she could arrange. She used all of her training in customer relations and psychology to help the gentleman understand that there simply were no planes taking off from any airport within a hundred mile radius, but the man nonetheless insisted, raising his voice and asking over and over again, "Do you know who I am? Do you know who I am?" She attempted to gently deflect the question, which to her mind had no relevant answer, but the man asked again, even more adamantly, "I asked you, do you know who I am?"

Exasperated, the airline representative took the microphone for the waiting area into her hand and said, "Ladies and gentlemen: May I have your attention for an important announcement, please? If anyone in the boarding area knows who this man is, please come forward. He keeps asking if I know who he is, and I do not. If anyone here knows, please come and help this man."

Sometimes Masters of the Universe need to be reminded of what the American Declaration of Independence articulated so memorably—namely, that all men are created equal; that is, they all possess the same dignity as human beings.

Sometimes all of us need to be reminded of it. Human reason can recognize the basic equality of human beings in the sense that there are no super-humans or sub-humans, but human beings also have a way of forgetting that important principle. In fact, most cultures in human history have been pretty good about hushing it up and brushing it under the carpet. The historical reality is that Judeo-Christian culture was the first to acknowledge human dignity in any widespread and institutional form.

This is largely the result of the biblical conception of the human person as created in the image of God, the understanding that God "made from one [man] every nation of men to live on all the face of the earth" (Acts 17:26), and the belief that in Christ there is "neither Jew nor Greek, there is neither slave nor free" (Galatians 3:28). The fact that Christianity was willing to baptize both slaves and aristocrats into the same church community changed society in a profound way.

This is not to say that a full-formed understanding of all the implications of this solidarity burst upon the world stage instantly upon the establishment of the Church, or that human equality was at all times and in all places understood and honored by every Christian. The recognition that human beings are equal worked its way into the fabric of Western civilization slowly and arduously, making advances here even while losing ground there. Or to use another metaphor, like a mighty river that begins as a trickle but eventually, over many centuries, carves valleys through mountains, this idea transformed the social landscapes of Europe and America slowly rather than all at once, but with the result that Western civilization was the first to get rid of slavery, and the first to extend suffrage to women.

Equal Respect, Not Equal Conditions

My favorite compliment after a speech (other than being commended by a teenager, especially after church, which is the highest possible compliment!) is being told that I have put into words what someone has thought for a long time but never been able to articulate. I often hear that when I relate this memory from my Brooklyn childhood.

Recall, I grew up in a family of six in a small apartment above Coney Island Avenue. Both my parents had jobs—my father spending blistering days on the roofs of various buildings spreading tar and laying the hot black paper; my mother waiting tables, doing factory work, and working as a cashier in a department store. We did not own a car in those days, to my memory, and I was the first of the siblings to grow up with a TV (a heavy brown box that got three stations, if you were lucky). We had enough to eat. I went to school, as had my siblings before me. If there were government handouts to be had, I never heard of them. I also never felt deprived. Far from it. As I love to tell people, you only had to walk down the one flight from our two-bedroom apartment and onto the busy avenue to put yourself in the middle of a spontaneous multi-ethnic experiment with a veritable smorgasbord of smells and accents and cultures all on display. Here we were, a diverse group in many ways but sharing certain traits in common. The households were, for the most part, headed by hard-working first- or second-generation immigrants all sweating their way up the economic ladder. There was absolutely no consciousness of poverty. Instead there was a lot of talk of "hustling," which did not have the same connotation of dishonesty as it does today. And besides, we had the Dodgers. (Though not for long. In those days, losing our team was what we thought impoverishment meant!)

We shared a sense of hopefulness, not because everything was easy or pleasant or because we all agreed with one another. Our hope was rooted in a shared belief in human capacity.

It is no coincidence that Marxism—what some have called the last Christian heresy, with its secularized doctrine of a brotherhood of man, its linear view of history, and its eschatology pointing toward a time of universal peace and happiness—sprang up not in India or China or Africa but in the culture of Christian Europe. Marx took a cluster of truths that Christianity taught about this world and the next, stripped them of their transcendental meaning, and then, as G. K. Chesterton might have said, went mad with them. Marxists saw sin as a mere social construct that could be purged by the historical dialectical process of class conflict and the eventual rise and dictatorship of the proletariat. Thus would heaven be brought down to earth—by as much force as necessary. The problem with Marxism, and many of its kissing cousins, is the anthropology—Marxists forget that one of the most important ways that human beings are equal is that we are *all* unique, precious, and unrepeatable—not indistinguishable cogs in a dialectical materialist progress machine.

Marxism took the true understanding of human equality and then utterly disfigured it, triggering injustice, oppression, and inequality on a scale that even its harshest early critics did not foresee. What is sadly fascinating is that, even after all the poverty and oppression that Marxism has demonstrably brought into the world, some of the seeds that Marx sowed are still sufficiently resilient to sprout in new hybrid forms today.

Marxism's less extreme cousins on the left took a less direct route to the same dead end. They anesthetized and emasculated their cultures by employing democratic processes to pursue equality at the expense of liberty and thus initiated the slower, less violent tragedies that we see unfolding in many European nations today. In Greece, Italy, Spain, and France people indignantly strike in outrage over being asked to work at least until the ripe old age of sixty-two, or being asked to face the fact that the state is not a limitless trough they can draw upon for unlimited health care, vacations, education, and other goods. In reality these things all cost money, money borrowed ultimately from Chinese workers and from future generations of the Europeans' own offspring—putting the generations not yet born into debt. Sadly, the United States has started down the same path.

There is a plain yet persistently misunderstood lesson here, one we would do well to heed before it is too late for the West: if equality is misunderstood and twisted or expanded beyond its nature, if it is made into an idol, then it becomes an instigator of class warfare and collective theft and discrimination against entire categories of people. The inevitable result is poverty, oppression, and misery, often on a grand scale.

For this reason it is of the utmost importance that we understand exactly how human beings are equal and how they are not, and what does and does not constitute an effective defense of true human equality. In law, recognizing equality means treating people impartially, without favoritism. It does not mean guaranteeing identical results.

There is a contradiction at the heart of the progressive project of striving toward equality of outcome by redistributing wealth. A tenacious focus on outcomes (as in redistribution to achieve income parity) inevitably leads to treating people unfairly—unequally—by taking from one who has worked and produced superfluous wealth, and giving it to one who has not.

And further, because equality as sameness is ultimately impossible to achieve, its pursuit tilts a society toward authoritarianism and totalitarianism, toward ever greater intrusions by the state in a vain attempt to maintain equality that is continually upset by different abilities, interests, and character traits. Enormous power comes to be concentrated in the hands of the politicians who are the arbiters of this equality, often leading to a most unequal society of political insiders and outsiders. In place of a culture of wealth makers (the entrepreneurs and their increasingly productive employees) you end up with a culture of wealth takers. The political class lives extravagantly off of the citizens without creating any new value—while undermining wealth creation among its citizens.

Social Justice and the Common Good

In countless debates and conversations with modern proponents of social justice, I have noticed that they are less interested in justice than in material equality. They borrow the language of justice and the common good but have either forgotten or rejected the classical meanings of those terms

In the classical tradition of reflection on justice (especially seen in Aristotle, St. Thomas Aquinas, and their intellectual descendants) it is clear that inequality—in the sense of unequal wealth or social status—is mostly compatible with justice, because justice is "to give to each his due." What one is due, of course, differs from person to person—in addition to those things due everyone: life, dignity, and liberty for example.

When we speak of the idea of the common good, we need to be open-minded about the most likely way to bring it about. The common good is, after all, a range of conditions, not a set of policies. It cannot be achieved by way of the "commonality of goods" proposed by socialists, but rather through the institutions that the socialists worked so hard to discredit. Let me list some of the conditions that are especially important for human flourishing: rule of law in the sense of courts acting in a non-arbitrary manner; secure private property in the means of production; stable money to serve as a reliable means of exchange; the freedom of enterprise that allows people to start businesses to pursue their dream; the freedom of association that permits people to reach mutually unforced agreements for employing or being employed; the enforcement of contracts to ensure that people keep their reasonable promises and that disputes are arbitrated justly; and vibrant trade within and among nations to permit the fullest possible flowering of the division of labor. These institutions must be supported by a culture that regards the human person as possessing an inherent dignity and creative potential, and believes that transcendent morality trumps the civil authority's attempt to redefine morality. This is the basis of what we call freedom, and it encourages what we call the common good.

The common good is incompatible with the violation of the right to economic initiative. And this isn't just a private idea of mine, or even something restricted to economists and Tea Party activists. I emphasize this fact because many people carry around the notion—perhaps only vaguely held—that any truly thoughtful and compassionate church leader takes a dim view of the free economy. For the sake of space, let me offer up just a single prominent counterexample. Pope John Paul II grew up under Soviet communism, and he also had plenty of opportunities to view the softer socialism of various Western European countries. He was deeply concerned with the poor and suffering of the world, as was evidenced both by his writings and his punishing travel schedule; he visited more developing countries than any pope before him. This is what John Paul wrote of economic initiative: "It is a right which is important not only for the individual but also for the common good. Experience shows us that the denial of this right, or its limitation in the name of an alleged 'equality' of everyone in society, diminishes, or in practice absolutely destroys the spirit of initiative, that is to say the creative subjectivity of the citizen."[4]

Unfortunately, many contemporary proponents of social justice miss the importance of economic freedom and are quick to denounce the profit motive and commercialism. They then compound their error with incoherence, since they seem to think the key to happiness is giving people more stuff—by enlisting the coercive power of government. Their exclusive focus on income and wealth as the sources and markers of equality is, ironically, merely another variety of the greed and consumerism that they are quick to excoriate. This is not really social justice; it's materialism. And it certainly isn't generosity, since these people's focus is on giving away *other people's* money.

True justice and the common good do not require equality in the sense of economic sameness. My friend and colleague Arthur Brooks, a social researcher who is now president of the American Enterprise Institute, has shown that what truly promotes human happiness is not unearned income but rather a system that frees and encourages earned success—a system, in other words, that doesn't multiply disincentives to achievement, doesn't suffocate ambition.[5]

If that is not a description of the market economy I do not know what is.

Places like China and India are experiencing incredible economic growth, and not because wealth has been redistributed. These countries have begun moving away from socialist political models, away from a single-minded emphasis on redistribution, and finally are allowing their citizens to begin creating wealth, and to keep most of the wealth they do manage to create. The two nations have a long way to go on the road to economic freedom, of course, but at least they appear to be headed in that direction—having learned the hard way the problems that result from denying their citizens that freedom.

The truly sad thing is that while the East was waking up to the blessings of economic freedom, much of Western Europe was being lulled asleep by the mirage of socialist redistribution and hyper-regulation. We're seeing the train wreck of the "social assistance state" in Europe today.

How is this for being prescient? In his 1991 social encyclical, *Centesimus Annus*, John Paul II warned that a bloated state "leads to a loss of human energies and an inordinate increase of public agencies, which are dominated more by bureaucratic thinking than by concerns for serving their clients, and which are accompanied by an enormous increase in spending." Those words aptly describe Western Europe today, particularly Greece, France, and Italy.

None of this is a call to embrace the greed-is-good mantra. We spent the last chapter slaying that dragon. Let's not have him rise from the dead here. Judeo-Christian morality minces no words in its condemnation of the idolatry of money and material goods. "The love of money is the root of all kinds of evil," St. Paul writes to Timothy. We must never make money our god. We must never permit the pursuit of material goods to obscure our obligations to God and neighbor. But there is an alternative to both consumerism and the anthropological confusion of socialism. That alternative neither condemns market activities nor exalts them beyond their rightful place in the grand scheme of things. Instead it calls us to work for the good of others and voluntarily contribute as we can of our time, talents, and wealth—the wealth that we have earned by serving others in a market economy. We must also work to build just systems of trade that enable the poor to be the agents of their own betterment, not merely grateful recipients of our generosity.

Economic prosperity is the result of people being allowed the freedom to engage in enterprise because when they do so they bring with them the whole of their knowledge, talent, experience, and character, and what emerges is a grand symphony of diversity (in other words, of all of those ways that human beings are unequal), an orchestration of talents, energies, needs, and interests, which may not have been the intention of any individual participant but is the result of all of them using their freedom.

If this sharing of energy and intelligence over the whole of society is not blocked and distorted by coercive intervention and manipulation by government, prosperity is the likely result. But the even greater benefit is that human beings are permitted to thrive, permitted to use their reason, courage, and imagination in positive ways not possible under economic tyranny, ways that bless them and others. This points toward a central purpose of our social order: to construct an institutional arrangement, under law, whereby man can truly become man's greatest resource.

Instead of focusing on equality of present material condition, then, we will do better to focus on a justice that recognizes the fundamental equality—the inherent dignity—of all people, but does not require that all people be equal in the way they look and act, nor that they possess exactly the same things. In this light, we can see that the free economy is a force for good. Both hard collectivism and soft collectivism drive society toward illusory forms of equality whose pursuit is destructive of both wealth and human freedom. The free economy respects our equal rights and equal dignity, and promotes the enhancement of personal initiative, and voluntary communal bonds—genuine social justice. The free economy is the enemy not of true equality, but of those bent on the acquisition of political and bureaucratic power. And it is the friend of true justice, extending economic freedom under the rule of law to rich and poor alike, because all are endowed by their Creator with certain unalienable rights.

Suggestions for Further Reading

Samuel Gregg, *The Commercial Society* (Lexington Books, 2007).

F. A. Hayek, *Law, Legislation, and Liberty*, vol. 2, *The Mirage of Social Justice* (University of Chicago, 1978).

Jennifer Roback Morse, "Defending the Weak and the Idol of Equality," *Religion and Liberty* 16 (Summer 2006), http://www.acton.org/pub/religion-liberty/volume-16-number-3/defending-weak-and-idol-equality.

CHAPTER 7

Why Smart Charity Works—and Welfare Doesn't

Q: Private charity is great, but it can't take care of all the needs out there. We can't let people in our society go without the basic necessities—food, medical care, a roof over their heads. Surely public assistance needs to be available as a last resort?

■ ■ ■

A: If only government assistance *were* a last resort! The displacement of charity by welfare has left people's most fundamental moral and spiritual needs unmet—and in the process actually perpetuated material poverty.

■ ■ ■

I have had the experience a thousand times: I get stopped on the street by an inebriated panhandler and asked for money. Whether I pull out a dollar or walk past avoiding his eye, it's an uncomfortable choice. As it turns out, there's actually a name for this problem—"the Samaritan's dilemma." A panhandler hits you up for money and giving to him feels like the big-hearted thing to do. But, particularly if the person shows signs of drug or alcohol abuse, something tells us that doing the generous thing may not be so smart. What do you do in a situation like that? Many people have "a heart for the poor." But if we really love the poor—if we want to see suffering humanity truly helped—we must acquire "a head for the poor" as well.

Applying our intelligence as well as our sympathy is actually the most loving thing we can do for the poor. We shouldn't live our lives based on our sentiments, or be guided mainly by what makes us feel good. Imagine what kind of world we would be living in if we approached all of life the way we too often approach charity—with a Lady Bountiful disposition, giving mostly to feel good about ourselves. If we let our feelings take control in other areas, our lives would soon become disordered, animalistic. If we are going to genuinely assist suffering humanity, our sentiments have to be disciplined—that is, made disciples of our reason. We need to think rationally and deliberately about how we approach the whole question of charity, which does not mean we need to be less passionate about it. And that begins with understanding what the human person is and isn't.

When animals are hungry or thirsty, we take them to the trough; when they are cold, we put them in the barn. But human beings are more than animals and need something more than what animals need. If we do not take this into consideration in the way we approach service to those in need, we will fail in our goal of helping the poor flourish as *human beings*. Besides, we will fail to respect the rich complexity of the human person. If we are to actually *do* good—not just *intend* good—we must look not only at the material wants and needs of the poor but also at their dignity, their capacity, and their unfulfilled spiritual needs—needs that sometimes are at the root of the dire material circumstances people find themselves in.

The Judeo-Christian culture knows something about all this. The belief that all human beings have the same origin and share a kinship deeper than even genetics allowed the idea of human solidarity to take root—the basic recognition of ourselves in others. I do not mean that this sense is completely absent until a person encounters the Christian message. Any passerby on the road who stops to assist at the scene of an accident is demonstrating the innate human sense of solidarity. This is something we might witness in almost any culture thanks to the workings of reason and grace (though, we may not realize, perhaps more in cultures historically shaped by Christianity). But Christianity awakened and invigorated this sense of human solidarity, not all at once but over the course of many centuries, working in sinful humanity like leaven in a lump of dough.

The evidence is in the history of Christian Europe. Christian civilization built the most extensive network of care for the vulnerable and needy the world had ever seen. Christendom, of course, was far from perfect. It was run by flawed and sinful humanity. And yet while critics of the West are only too happy to dwell endlessly on every human evil in the history of Christendom, we would do well to remember the other side of the coin: such things as hospitals, social service agencies, orphanages, networks of schools, and globalized charity (not to mention universities and modern science) simply did not exist as institutions until Christianity entered human history and gradually transformed Western civilization.

Desiccated Compassion

The charitable institutions we take for granted all come out of the Judeo-Christian tradition's profound respect for the individual human person who is invested with an innate dignity. The tragedy is that today the welfare state in the West is only a secularized, materialistic, and desiccated form of a richer, more personal, and more effective form of compassion. That human solidarity was rooted in a love so potent that it inspired armies of men and women to abandon the familiarity of home and family to seek out and save (in both the material and spiritual sense) those who were lost.

The modern welfare state, in contrast, hardly inspires anyone—whether the recipient or the provider—to do anything. Instead of neighbor acting on behalf of neighbor in need, we have clients of unwilling benefactors—on the one hand, people who are the receptacles of services, on the other hand, taxpayers coerced into supporting those services. And neither the "donors" nor the beneficiaries have probably ever even met each other. In place of generous souls animated by love of neighbor, we see a soulless bureaucracy run by distant bureaucrats and funded by politicians seeking out constituents by promising benefits—a system that, in the words of Pope Benedict XVI, "ultimately become[s] a mere bureaucracy incapable of guaranteeing the very thing which the suffering person—every person—needs: namely, loving personal concern."[1]

This is not to say that those who staff government social service agencies are not genuinely concerned about those they serve. Over the years I have come to know many within the bureaucracy who are the most dedicated and well-meaning people—and also the most hamstrung by the one-size-fits-all policies and bureaucratic rules that prevent real charity individually tailored to each person's needs. Bureaucracy inevitably separates people with good intentions from people with needs, so that the people being aided become less and less personally known to those supplying the aid.

This situation is partly due to the ideology behind the welfare state. Though it's not widely known, Marxists and even non-Marxist architects of the welfare state have typically opposed face-to-face personalized private charity, believing that almsgiving is nothing more than a way for the rich to shirk their obligations to justice and to anesthetize the poor to their misery—calming their revolutionary impulses. In fact, *The Communist Manifesto* dismisses the whole of philanthropy in a sentence, saying "the bourgeoisie is desirous of redressing social grievances, in order to secure the continued existence of bourgeois society." Non-Marxist progressives have typically shared this dim view of charity. L. A. Halbert, the superintendent of the first municipal Board of Public Welfare in the United States (established in Kansas City, in 1910) touted the depersonalization of government-provided welfare as a virtue: "relief becomes merely a business transaction and the element of charity is entirely eliminated."[2] In the socialist vision, wide-spread government redistribution replaces private charity by ensuring that the working classes and the poor do not have to depend on benevolence. Paying taxes replaces individual involvement in charitable work, and the state becomes the charitable resource of first resort, crowding out the traditional institutions that once cared for the vulnerable.[3]

And the traditional institutions crowded out by welfare aren't just churches and charities—they also include the family itself. For example, when the state reaches out to help children by providing a hot breakfast or an after-school program, so that schools become more congenial and dependable zones of comfort and care than the home, one effect is to reduce the responsibility and value of parents to their own children and vice versa. It feels good to give poor kids free meals at school, but is it good for the families in poor communities? Are there other ways to meet the needs of families that have trouble providing nutrition to their children? The problem becomes especially acute when welfare programs designed to benefit children positively discourage fathers' involvement in the family. In many cases state assistance not only replaces the father's role as protector and provider but, going still further, creates perverse incentives for single mothers to *avoid* marriage—never mind that marriage provides substantial benefits to women and children, including some that the state is incapable of providing. Welfare reform in the 1990s addressed some of these perverse incentives, but much of that reform was rolled back in the American Recovery and Reinvestment Act of 2009 (the "stimulus" bill).[4] As so often happens, good policy gave way to tricky politics.

The perverse structure of the welfare system helps to explain why poor Americans are now less likely than wealthy Americans to marry and form sustained, intact families. As sociologist Stewart Tolnay put it, "One does not need to embrace the conservatives' nearly exclusive emphasis on welfare policy as the cause of non-marital childbearing to acknowledge that government policies are an active ingredient in the stew of macro-level forces that influence individual family-related behavior."[5] Yale University sociologist Elijah Anderson is less cautious: "It has become increasingly socially acceptable for a young woman to have children out of wedlock—significantly, with the help of a regular welfare check."[6]

Government Isn't the Only Institution

Proponents of the Welfare State have a point when they claim that not all of society's needs can be met by the market alone. To say that there is room for other institutions in addressing those needs is an understatement; it is imperative for the well-being of a nation's citizens that there exist a vibrant set of what Alexis de Tocqueville identified as "mediating institutions"—groups that occupy the space between the individual and the state. In the United States and in much of Western civilization, the Christian church has been a vital—one might argue the most significant—mediating institution.

The beneficial role that the church has played in the charitable sphere throughout history is today at risk from two distinct but related threats. When people of faith fail to build and support strong families, to provide charitable assistance to those in need, to address the moral and spiritual dimensions of the social pathologies that are often at the root of poverty and crime, their failure creates a vacuum into which the power of the state is drawn. Then government programs that attempt to replace what the church should be doing, or complicate her attempts to do charity in the world, in turn inevitably further the decay of religious organizations—either by co-opting them so as to render them merely instruments of state authority, or by actually forcing them out of public life altogether.

If government welfare were an adequate substitute for religious charity, there might be little problem with this scenario. But the differences between the two should lead us to be gravely concerned about the ways in which government is co-opting religious charities or forcing them out of the public square. State welfare is always prey to the inertia that historically infects almost all bureaucracies, the distance between policy planners and the specific problems that they formulate their cookie-cutter plans to address, and the fact that the political process is driven by people's interests, not their generous concern for the poor. All these inherent limitations of government welfare suggest that the state should not be the solution of first resort when it comes to poverty.

The solution of first resort ought to be religious charity. Here let me speak from a specifically Christian point of view with regard to the poor and vulnerable. In the Christian tradition, every human person is of unique and individual value. Compassion is not a Christian monopoly; human solidarity is a universal human trait, something encoded in us. But Christian charity (which is a *command* rather than an optional extra for the disciple of Christ) is more than philanthropy. Compassion has come to mean *giving to*, but as a fine researcher, Marvin Olasky, has pointed out, the word really means *suffering with*.[7] Christianity, the religion of the Suffering Servant, gets this. As Mother Teresa once so vividly put it, to encounter the poor (in all senses of poverty, not solely the material), is to encounter "Christ in distressing disguise."

Desiccated Christianity

It's important to emphasize this Christological dimension of Christian charity because many Christian agencies and even whole religious orders of consecrated men and women, originally founded on the basis of this original Christian inspiration, appear to have settled for a kind of Christian gloss over charitable work that is secular at its core. These religious communities have unwittingly allowed themselves to be guided by a kind of materialist framework for helping the poor. Such groups would do well to understand that Mother Teresa's words are not an expression of mere sentiment or outdated piety. They are a reflection of a core Christian idea, one that inspired those armies of missionaries who sought out "the lost"—so as to tend their material needs, certainly, but also to share the message of eternal life in Christ. Their great sacrifice, heroism, ingenuity and generosity flowed from their understanding of their mission—they were more than social workers; they were bearers of the eternal Good News.

And they were bringing that good news to human beings whom they saw as more than a bundle of unmet needs. They knew that the poor they served had eternal souls more valuable than the most prized possessions of the rich. The English writer C. S. Lewis captures the spirit of their anthropology with a striking image: "Next to the Blessed Sacrament itself your neighbor is the holiest object presented to your senses."[8]

When Christian institutions attempt to mitigate or compromise this understanding of their mission—often as the result of the political pressure—they morph into shadowy versions of their former selves. Often instead of a passion for the Faith a substitute passion comes into play—a passionate political agenda which attempts to bring the kingdom of God to earth through political means. Dissent if you like from any proposition of the Nicene Creed, but not from any piece of legislation funding welfare budgets. That, to their minds, is the *real* heresy!

The reasons for the secularization of religious institutions are undoubtedly many, but among them one can identify the loss of confidence in the message of the Gospel in the face of secular social science. In the popular imagination one sees the budding of this mindset in Harvey Cox's *The Secular City* (1965), followed by other corruptions of orthodox Christianity by the secularist ideology that underlay, for example, most forms of Liberation theology and Feminist theology. These movements called into question the whole manner in which theology had been done over the preceding 2000 years, introducing a skepticism about traditional faith, which their adherents believed needed to be corrected by Marxist social analysis or feminist critiques of "patriarchy" in the church. What all this boiled down to in the pew was a sense that somehow religion had to "get with it" in order to "be relevant" to what was going on in the culture.

By the 1990s, the decline of mainline Protestantism was obvious—and documented by Thomas Reeves in *The Empty Church*. The sad irony is that the very churches most willing to compromise in pursuit of being "hip" or "culturally relevant" were the very ones that suffered the greatest decline in membership among the young. The Episcopalian, Presbyterian, and Methodist denominations, known in recent decades for their ardent pursuit of "relevancy," barely managed to retain 50 percent of their minor members into adulthood."[9] The situation has not improved in the years since. Instead decline has spread to other churches, most noticeably the single largest religious body in America, the Catholic Church. Regular Mass attendance has fallen from more than 60 percent in 1960 to less than 30 percent today. Some 10 percent of *all Americans* are ex-Roman Catholics.[10]

These figures are not of interest only to churchgoers; the decline in religious life has had pernicious effects on American culture more broadly. At the same time that most nuns were abandoning their habits and some priests their collars, when overtly Christian terminology and symbols were dropped from the names and descriptions of various Christian organizations in an attempt "not to alienate any one," and when ministers began focusing their attention on liberal political causes rather than preaching the Gospel message of repentance and salvation, a widespread cultural decline also emerged, one marked by growing hostility toward parental, political, and religious authority; a rise in drug use; and skyrocketing rates of divorce and out-of-wedlock births.

What I find remarkable is that this trend should surprise anyone. The heart of a healthy Judeo-Christian culture is that locus of unifying ideas that sustains and inspires respect for the divine and the beings made in his image. If those ideas are somehow called into question or secularized, it follows that the culture will change.

And that decline has been particularly hard on the poor in America. Climbing out of poverty and staying out of poverty involves a measure of good fortune, certainly, but it also requires hope and confidence, along with a sense of responsibility, a work ethic, honesty, temperance, and all the other virtues that enable individuals to thrive. This isn't to say there aren't hard-working and virtuous poor people. Of course there are—I grew up with many of them. But when the institutions that teach, model, and reiterate the importance of these virtues are weakened or absent, then, all other things being equal, poverty becomes easier to fall into and harder to climb out of.[11]

The Mayor of My Neighborhood

People from across the political spectrum would generally nod their heads at the idea that when seeking to help the poor we need to address the whole person. But most people have yet to think through the policy implications of that principle. None of the virtues that I have outlined above lend themselves to transmission by an automated, faceless process. They can't be phoned in or transmitted through glossy textbooks or high-speed internet or iPads in every student backpack—or even by a cadre of well-intentioned politicians in Washington. Truly serving the poor—helping them tap their own potential, rather than treating them as nothing more than mouths to feed—requires the personal attention of people deeply concerned for those in need.

For me nothing better illustrates this point than a nosy little woman who lived on my block in Brooklyn when I was a boy. When I have shared my memory of Mrs. Rabinowitz with audiences around the world, I am repeatedly told that she didn't just live in Brooklyn, but everywhere.

My mother referred to Mrs. Rabinowitz as the "Mayor of the Neighborhood." From her stoop (Brooklyn had no porches, only stoops) she could survey the block from one end to the other with an eye out for anything curious, unusual, or amiss. There she would be atop her perch on a summer's day as my friends and I played stickball in the narrow street. Home base was a manhole cover; first base was an old Rambler with a rumble seat in the back. Second was another manhole cover and third base was the Deering's 1955 Studebaker Lark Daytona Wagonaire (which they needed, with their seven kids). Ten or twelve boys would work up a sweat and exchange taunts, but if any of us began to really get out of line Mrs. Rabinowitz's voice would go off like a siren. She needed only to pronounce one of our names, and she would bring whatever scuffle had broken out to a compete standstill.

How could a nosy old Jewish woman bring order out of the chaos of a gaggle of teenage boys? Could such a thing happen in that neighborhood today? It is unlikely. Mrs. Rabinowitz possessed an implicit authority that demanded that we yield to her: she was the eyes and ears of the community, the enforcer of a moral code that was not up for grabs but widely shared among the parents and business owners of the community. In Brooklyn in the early 1960s we did not have to reinvent morality from scratch in the face of every new temptation. For example, when an adult addressed a child, the child was expected to respond. I have no specific memory of ever having been taught this as a child. It was just something that my friends and I knew.

Mrs. Rabinowitz's age demanded respect. We understood that to contradict the orders of an elderly matron was in some way to disrespect those whose authority over us was more direct—our own parents. And it did not hurt at all that she knew our parents personally, and that one word to them that we were causing trouble would result in real unpleasantness.

In any case, it worked. Mrs. Rabinowitz could bring order out of chaos; she could govern without government. What her one-word warning could achieve then would take a squadron of police to achieve today.

And here we can discern a critical principle of economics. Academic economists call it "the knowledge problem": when policy planners gather to resolve some kind of social or economic problem—for example, the persistent problem of urban teenage boys acting up on the street—these planners generally commission studies to determine what the society's problems are and how to resolve them. They compile statistics about the income levels and the demographic characteristics of the poor. They arrive at a fairly accurate picture of poverty as a social problem—from a bird's eye view. In the best case, they even differentiate various sorts of poverty and try to address them with programs taking various approaches—food stamps deal with hunger, CHIP assists with children's health care, and TANF offers income support to needy families. But poverty does not happen at a bird's eye level. It happens to individual people and families who are as diverse as the human race itself.

The Fatal Welfare Conceit

The practical implication of the overwhelming diversity of human beings and situations is that however much the planners try to account for variety, they cannot possibly address from their offices in Washington the nearly infinite array of problems and needs that poor people have. The functional single mother who works part-time does not need the same help as the drug-addicted single mother who barters every form of public assistance to feed her habit. If distant bureaucrats are capable of missing a difference as stark as this, how much more will they fail to make the far subtler distinctions among the various people on their welfare rolls—differences inherently resistant to statistical analysis and bureaucratic categorization but essential to the work of providing effective compassion?

The problem is not the intentions of the central planners (although this is always something to watch in politics). The problem is their lack of real information, the missing local knowledge. Bureaucrats usually know less than they think they know, and they never know enough of what needs to be known. And they always know less than Mrs. Rabinowitz.

The information problem is compounded when the planners do not even know that they face an insurmountable information problem. Nobel Laureate and economist Friedrich Hayek called this the "synoptic delusion" or "the fatal conceit." The synoptic (one-eyed) delusion is the notion that a single analyst—not necessarily a single individual, but a single entity or agency—can accurately comprehend and assess the entire range of information necessary to predictably manipulate a complex social organism such as a modern culture or economy. The synoptic delusion is closely related to what economists call the law of unintended consequences. Because policy-makers can never have perfect knowledge about the people their policies affect, for every economic intervention (such as a government welfare policy), there will be effects that are neither intended nor guessed by those who designed the policy.

Hayek was formalizing what should be common sense. After all, how plausible is it that a small group of people, attempting to design a response to a highly complex social dilemma such as poverty in a distant neighborhood, are really going to have at hand all the relevant facts and knowledge to actually be able to do good? Certainly, statisticians can supply helpful data. For example, they can tell us that 40.7 percent of female-headed households with children but no husband and father live in poverty, while only 8.8 percent of married-family households are poor.[12] But how do you actually help the women who are or who may become trapped in this kind of at-risk family type? The bureaucratic mentality tends to commission studies, assemble committees, develop an impersonal plan suited to numbers but not people, whereas the caring neighbor simply sees, listens, and acts.

Of course there are situations where an outside "rescuer" is needed. But even in these exceptional situations, there is often somebody who can help who is far closer to the problem than a bureaucrat in the state or national capitol. The Catholic principle of subsidiarity holds that needs are best met locally, and that higher levels of the social order should be careful not to interfere with lower orders, helping only when necessary and doing so in a way that is temporary and supportive.[13] The principle of subsidiarity means encouraging the Mrs. Rabinowitzes of a community—that is, the people and private charitable energies embedded in a community—rather than displacing them.

If you have some need—say you do not have sufficient money to pay your rent—the first level of responsibility for meeting that need is yours—you should get a job, or dip into your savings. But let's say you have broken your legs, do not have any savings, and cannot work. Who has the next level of responsibility to help you? Naturally, your family—your spouse or parents or siblings or extended family and close friends. They are closest to you and know you best. They know whether you really broke your legs or are just faking it. They may also know other details that it might be hard for strangers to know—or for bureaucrats to work into welfare benefit calculations: whether you fell down the stairs and broke your legs in a freak accident, or because you were kindly helping a friend move furniture, or because you were drunk, or because of the onset of Alzheimer's disease. And yet those circumstances of your accident are highly relevant to the question of what kind of help you actually need. Your family and friends may also know other people who know you or who would be moved, once they heard your story, to help in assisting you.

If there is no family support forthcoming, then maybe there are neighbors who are able and willing to assist. A church or other social organization to which you belong may be able to help. Ask any pastor: the easiest money to raise is a collection to alleviate a tragedy the people in the congregation know something about personally or feel personally connected to. There may be civic associations or charitable organizations designed to aid people in your specific situation.

And so on up the social ladder. On this model, there are a lot of rungs to climb before one reaches even the city level of government—and still more before one reaches the level of state and national government. It's fashionable these days to talk about agricultural localism (often while sitting in a Starbucks in Manhattan sipping gourmet coffee from halfway around the world). It's time we started talking more about charitable localism. It was precisely this kind of locally embedded social engagement that de Tocqueville saw in operation when he visited the United Sates in the 1830s, observing that "Americans of all ages, all conditions, and all dispositions, constantly form associations."[14]

The America of the 1830s had its problems of course, some of them shocking by today's standards. We shouldn't view the past too nostalgically. But we can recognize the problems of the past without muddling things. People often fail to appreciate the charitable culture that has been lost because they conflate the cultural charity of that age with its level of technological progress and standard of living, both of which were far below ours today. But we are not richer today because we began to soak our poor neighborhoods with government welfare. We live longer, materially richer lives today because 190 years of capitalist innovation has raised the standard of living to the point that today's poor can live better than upper middle class of even a hundred years ago. And in the midst of all this plenty, the neighborhoods in this country that have been flooded with government largesse are experiencing a very stubborn variety of poverty.

Leftists tend to criticize the private, localist approach to charity as "too individualistic" and corrosive to the social fabric. But subsidiarity is actually very respectful of the authentic social relationships and local knowledge that people have of one another: it is not individualistic, but *personalistic.* In practice government welfare—not subsidiarity and local charity—tends to undermine community and accelerate the atomization of society.

To hold to the principle of subsidiarity is not to say that the government is never needed, or that government itself is evil, but merely that government should be a means of last resort in the face of most social problems, not of first resort. Government is primarily necessary to provide justice and to maintain the rule of law, so that the weak are not at the mercy of the strong. If it does all those things, government creates a context in which communities and society as a whole can flourish. But government power is like a sharp scalpel; if not wielded by a skilled and disciplined surgeon who knows both his role and his limitations, it is a dangerous weapon.

A common objection to the argument for depending on private and local charities as over against government welfare is that it "simply cannot work." Marvin Olasky has responded to this objection by documenting the extraordinary service rendered in the course of American history by non-governmental charitable organizations.[15] We see the same approach in the writings of St. Paul, who repeatedly admonished the churches under his authority to be generous to those in need—widows, orphans and the like. Paul also knew human nature and wisely warned, "If any one will not work, let him not eat."[16] He even warned one church not to provide a daily distribution of food to young, able-bodied widows lest they become idlers, gossips, and busybodies.[17] Paul's understanding of the dangers of indiscriminate charity underscores again the need for local knowledge. Is the person lazy or simply incapable and in need of job training or some other form of support? A family or church, which actually knows the person, has the ability to discern the answer. A distant bureaucrat probably does not.

Welfare: Four Threats to the Church

An expansive secular system of government charity poses several threats to religious bodies, especially to those that become dependent on government subsidies. Here are four major threats to the health of charitable religious bodies today:

1. The burgeoning welfare state hinders the church from fulfilling an essential part of its own mission as servant to the world, at times relegating the church to the role of a lobbyist and making it vulnerable to pressure from secularists in the political arena.
2. To the extent that the church functions as just another lobbyist instead of clothing the naked, feeding the hungry, and carrying out the other traditional acts of mercy as it has for 2000 years, it loses a rich source of its own spiritual nourishment—proximity to "Christ in a distressing disguise."
3. When the church becomes dependent on secular governments that are increasingly hostile to religion, many of the agencies operated by religiously affiliated institutions lose their moral rudder and cease to have a moral impact that can ameliorate the underlying moral and spiritual causes of economic poverty.
4. When people realize that they can rely on the state to meet human needs, a society's moral core is eroded as even Christians' incentive to personally help others diminishes and they cease to see themselves as personal, moral actors on behalf of those in need.

The Samaritan

The Marxist political analysis that remains popular (if now usually disguised) in many of our universities and even some seminaries, tends to pit the poor against the rich—it's all about class warfare and alienation. The alternative vision that I have been trying to paint in these pages is beautifully distilled in the parable of the Good Samaritan, a story that has held a persistent fascination for religious and non-religious readers alike. Of course, like all the parables, its primary meaning is Christological and moral, rather than political. But it's also possible to discern other less-noticed messages in this story.

In Luke's Gospel, a Samaritan man (someone on the margins of Jewish society in this period) stops to help a man who was beaten and left for dead on the side of the road. When this Samaritan comes upon him, he helps the beaten man from his own resources. Even when the Samaritan has to delegate the care of the man for a time to an innkeeper, he promises to pay the innkeeper back. The Samaritan was on the scene to see and understand the fallen man's specific needs—he was the man's "neighbor"—and he went about meeting those needs. From this standpoint, the Samaritan might be justly described as the principle of subsidiarity in action. Notice, too, that he would have been hard-pressed to meet the needs of the injured man if he hadn't first possessed enough personal wealth to hire the services of the innkeeper. Lady Thatcher's memorable insight about this text is to the point: "No one would remember the Good Samaritan if he'd only had good intentions; he had money as well."

Suggestions for Further Reading

Arthur C. Brooks, *Who Really Cares: The Surprising Truth About Compassionate Conservatism* (Basic Books, 2007).

David T. Beito, *From Mutual Aid to the Welfare State: Fraternal Societies and Social Services, 1890–1967* (University of North Carolina Press, 1999).

Theodore Dalrymple, *Life at the Bottom* (Ivan R. Dee, 2001).

Charles Murray, *Losing Ground: American Social Policy, 1950–1980, 10th Anniversary Edition* (Basic Books 1994).

Marvin Olasky, *The Tragedy of American Compassion* (Regnery, 1995).

CHAPTER 8

The Health of Nations: Why State-Sponsored Health Care Is Not Compassionate

Q: People need health care. Shouldn't government guarantee it? Don't the terrible inefficiencies and inequities in the current system prove that the only feasible way to provide health care to all is for government to run the system?

■ ■ ■

A: Most of the problems in the American health care system stem from government intervention, not from market failure. The fact is, we do not have a market-based health care system in America today, and we haven't had one for decades. If government, which currently pays for about half the medical care in the United States (and also heavily regulates private insurance), would get out of the way, we could have a health care system as innovative and efficient as the computer industry—with regular price cuts, instead of ever-rising costs. But setting aside questions of innovation and costs, we need to remember that the most profound care lies beyond the government and the market—in the realm of personal relationship and love.

■ ■ ■

Health care is an extraordinarily complex challenge, and good people can disagree about how best to address it. Thus, a first helpful move in the debate is to forego accusing the other side of bad faith. Not all advocates of government programs are intending to socialize medicine as a step down the path to totalitarianism. Not all proponents of market-oriented reform want to cast aside the sick and the elderly in pursuit of profit.

It's also important to keep in view—amidst all of the data about insurance costs, budget deficits, the percentages of doctors entering and leaving the profession, and the millions of other statistics that help us get a handle on the problem—the simple but easily forgotten fact that the principal subject of health care is not a statistic, but the human being. I have been in and out of too many emergency rooms not to understand how easy it is in the midst of our wondrous technology to forget that there is a human being under all that machinery. The patient caught up in the machinery, surrounded by all the beeps may even now be wondering if these are his last moments on earth: is this the place from which he will enter eternity? He may be experiencing regrets or recounting joys even as the nurses and doctors are busy drawing blood, taking his temperature, injecting painkillers, and checking blood pressure.

Of course, the problem of treating the sick callously has been with us as long as sickness and death have been with us. But today we say the health care system is in crisis. The rising cost of health care coverage is alarming. Spending on health care as a percentage of GDP was about 7 percent in 1970. It was fully 17 percent in 2011 ($2.7 trillion) and is projected to rise past 20 percent within the next ten years.[1]

These national statistics underscore the problem, but they can also obscure the fact that the crisis is playing out in countless personal struggles all across America. As health insurance costs continue to rise, working families who could once afford private health insurance find themselves dropping off the rolls and wondering how they'll afford the medical bills if somebody in their family gets really sick.

But while rapid price inflation is a serious problem, it isn't the root of the problem. It's a symptom of something deeper. Getting to the root of the problem is important, lest we concoct a remedy worse than the disease.

Fighting a Fire with Gasoline

Many attribute runaway health care costs to expensive new kinds of treatment or improved pharmaceuticals, but this explanation doesn't take us very far. The market for any number of new kinds of medical procedures and the technology that supports them is actually characterized by *falling* prices, particularly non-essential, elective procedures such as LASIK, cosmetic surgery, and health care for pets.

The three things that all of these have in common are (1) they are not heavily regulated by the government, (2) they are not subsidized by our tax dollars, and (3) they are not usually covered by insurance. In other words, people have to pay out of their own pocket for these kinds of health care, and the economy of buyers and sellers is relatively free of government coercion. Unfortunately the same cannot be said for most other medical services in America today. Government involvement in those other medical services, as we will see in due course, has a great deal to do with the present crisis in health care. The last thing we want to do is try to fix the problem by expanding government regulation, extending taxpayer subsidies, and increasing the number of routine procedures that insurance pays for. You don't put out a gasoline fire by pouring more gasoline on it.

Price, Profit, and Cost

We have already discussed how certain limitations necessarily flow from the stubborn fact of scarcity. Wilhelm Röpke, one of the economists behind the post-World War II "German Miracle," said, "The economist comes before his fellow citizens with the bad news of scarcity—as the production of goods increases, so does demand and desire—hence the

Kingdom of God will never come to earth through economic means."[2] This fundamental economic reality exists in every economic system under the sun, and applies to health care as well. Medical care does not appear out of nowhere. The amount of time needed for doctors, nurses, researchers, and administrators to complete their training and then actually deliver care to patients is not unlimited. Medicines, hospitals, and new technology are not in infinite supply, either. The result is that none of these things come without cost—and we must calculate the costs on some rational basis.

It would be a beautiful thing indeed if we could just skip over the annoying fact of scarcity—if you could just take what you need, when you need it, and at the level and quality you need. But in the real world, what would occur if we did ignore the reality of scarcity? We do not have to guess at the answer. The available resources would be quickly exhausted. Here I always think of that line from Thomas Henry Huxley: "A beautiful theory, killed by a nasty, ugly, little fact."

That nasty, ugly, little fact is scarcity. If you overlook the fundamental problem of scarcity, it's easy to fall into the trap of imagining that the problems in health care are all about greedy fat cats hogging something—just as filmmaker Michael Moore has done. In his film *SiCKO*, Moore calls for the complete end to private health care and excoriates profit as intrinsically evil. His ideas may sound radical, but he isn't alone. *Sojourners*, PICO National Network, the Center for Faith and Public Life, Faithful America, and Catholics in Alliance for the Common Good chimed in to advocate for more extensive government involvement and a further diminution of the role of profits in health care.

Ask any number of religious leaders, and they will tell you that competition in health care (as in education, by the way) is essentially immoral. How could any moral person, they argue, favor people making money off the sickness of others? They don't stop to consider that anyone who sells anything profitably in a market is in some sense making money off the "dis-ease"—the lack or insufficiency—of others. The home builder is making money off the homelessness of home buyers; clothing manufacturers off the nakedness of clothing buyers; restaurants off the hunger of diners.

But isn't medical care different? Well, it does strike closer to the bone, so to speak. It is a matter of life and death. Of course each of these goods—shelter, clothing, and, especially and more immediately, food—can be matters of life and death in extreme circumstances. And the same is true of medical care. Not every procedure is necessary, not every procedure is necessary immediately and, even where a procedure is necessary right now, the patient's need is no justification for making indentured servants of the skilled professionals who are able to provide the service. Far from it. That need is rather a call to respect the professionals who can fill it, to offer them market rates for their skill and their years of hard work developing and honing it.

Do we really want to embrace the alternative to a free market in medicine? If profits and cost-benefit analyses are allowed to play no role whatsoever in the way we calculate health care provision, then doctors, nurses, and the vast array of support personnel will no longer be allowed to calculate the costs of their time in the care and support of the sick *vis-à-vis* their personal responsibilities at home. What about their right to a just return for their labor? Does this same prohibition apply to the researchers and developers of new technologies and medicines? Without profits, how will we prevent them from choosing to devote their time to more remunerative work? Are we prepared to turn our medical doctors and nurses into highly skilled slaves to keep them on task?

I am not asking these questions because anyone in Washington is proposing to pack all of our heart surgeons, knee doctors, and surgical nurses into little slave cabins and force them to work ninety-hour weeks for Ramen noodles and tap water (though I'm told that this pretty accurately describes the life of a medical student). The point of the question is to highlight the incoherence of calls to banish profit from health care. What this impulse effectively amounts to is the desire to put government bureaucrats in charge of who gets paid what for this or that service.

A profit-free health care system is a chimera. The central problem in the United States isn't doctors and nurses putting in years of demanding training in the hopes of making a good living. That's how we end up with plenty of doctors and nurses! The problem is the dominance of third party payment throughout the health care system. Few Americans pay their medical costs directly. About half of health care expenses are paid for by government programs, and the bulk of the rest are covered by private insurance plans purchased by employers. This separation between the payer and the consumer is at the root of most of the problems of our health care system—including rising costs.

When we walk into almost any store—whether to buy shoes or ketchup or towels—we tend to engage in comparisons. We estimate the value of each brand based on personal experience and reports from other people on its reliability, quality, and cost-to-value ratio. If we're making a particularly important or costly purchase, we may do some additional research in Consumer Reports or, increasingly, on the internet. Where markets are competitive, such consumer resources are generated naturally because there is demand for them.

Human cooperation along these lines is a marvelous thing. Take, for example, the Internet Movie Database (imdb.com). Millions of visitors voluntarily post synopses, rate movies, and offer parental advisory material, providing a trove of information to other visitors at no charge. Similarly, there are various gas price web sites giving motorists up-to-date information in their quest for the most inexpensive fill-up in the area.

So here's the question: why is there nothing like these sites for our medical care? And honestly, when was the last time you asked your doctor for the cost of any procedure he proposed? Rarely do we even know the true cost of a visit to the doctor's office. And do we care? Most of us do not because our insurance companies—not we—pay the bill.

But of course we ultimately do pay for health care—at prices inflated by the fact that nobody can see the prices and shop carefully for it. Our salaries are thousands of dollars less than they might be were our employers not faced with massive health insurance premium increases every year. And our income tax bills—not to mention our growing national debt—are higher than they would be if tens of millions of Americans were not dependent on Medicare and Medicaid, which are even more insulated from personal cost considerations than company-provided health insurance. The deplorable lack of knowledge we have about the real cost of the medical care we choose is the single greatest reason for the unsustainably steep climb in health care prices. We cannot go on at this rate forever. Something has to change.

Let Them Compete

We have been talking about the essential role of profits. There is an even clearer way of thinking about what's missing from the current system, but it's going to force us to use two other dirty words—*competition* and *prices*. If your idea of market competition is the law of the jungle, or vicious wolves eating sweet little old grannies, please bear with me for a moment. I am not referring to vicious woodland predators competing for adorable bunnies. I'm referring to sellers competing for the sweet little granny's business by bidding against one another to provide the best medical services at the best value. I know that isn't half as theatrical or interesting as Little Red Riding Hood, but that's what I mean when I say that the current health care system is desperately in need of competition. We need competition under the rule of law, of course—sellers competing for buyers in a market governed by laws against bullying, theft, and deception—the sort of competition you get in a properly free economy. The problem is that there is precious little of this kind of competition in the health care sector in America today.

If this claim sounds overblown, ask yourself a question: when was the last time you saw gasoline for sale at one price on one corner, and then at three or four times that price a few blocks away. I don't mean 3 or 4 cents more expensive. I mean, three or four times as expensive. You never see that because there is free and transparent competition for customers in the gasoline market across America; customers are spending their own money, and they know the full cost of the gasoline they are buying. The situation is very different in our health care system. It is not unusual for the cost of the same treatment or procedure to differ significantly from doctor to doctor and from hospital to hospital. One study completed in 2011 found some extreme cases: a pelvic CT scan cost $230 at one facility and $1800 at another—in the same town![3]

Of course there are differences in quality. But I'm sorry, you can add bells and whistles to a CT scan all day and it won't make it worth *eight times* the cost of the CT scan down the street. These massive price variations are telling us something: the price signals in our health care system have been buried under a cacophony of noise.

They're also telling us that something is standing in the way of free competition. When competition is absent—when one seller or one buyer dominates the market and new vendors or consumers are prevented from entering—then the price does not reliably reflect actual supply and demand. Prices are not serving as a signal for people to buy less of one thing and more of another, or for producers to make more of one thing or less of another. This is the kind of situation that prevailed over the whole economy of the Soviet Union—so that there were always too many or too few goods on the shelves of Soviet shops.

Competition involves a contest of rivals, in the sense that it provides rival, or alternative, products to consumers. It is rivalrous, but it is also cooperative since it's a way of coordinating economic activity without relying upon a central planner. With competition in a free market, planning comes not from one center of special interest, knowledge or authority, but from the knowledge, needs, and interests of individuals who are dispersed over the whole of society.[4] Competition peaceably coordinates a market of business people, incentivized largely though not exclusively by the potential profits to be made by bringing to market a good or service that people want or need. This process focuses many minds on people's desires and necessities, and puts many hands to work supplying them.

Big Brother, Big Burden

But what about life-saving medical services that are simply too expensive for some people to afford? Scarcity is a harsh mistress, especially when you're dealing with a life-and-death resource. What we have to keep squarely in view, though, is that socialized health care is neither a compassionate nor an effective solution. Socialized medicine undermines compassion by setting the state between the individual and his doctor, leading to dehumanized conditions for both patient and provider—long lines, endless paperwork, and top-down bureaucratic rationing. It is not a good state of affairs when medical providers come to see the government, rather than the patient, as their primary client. A socialized health care system also undermines technological innovation, just as a government takeover of any realm of the economy suffocates innovation—by severing the free relationship among buyers and sellers, crushing incentives for excellence, and bogging down potential innovators and providers in a thicket of regulation.

How many of us know physicians who have retired early because they were sick of dealing with labyrinthine federal regulations handed down by distant bureaucrats without a tenth of the medical training of the physicians? The government attempts to distribute scarce health care resources without allowing a free market to set prices—and ends up creating more scarcity as it drives a physician's career into an early grave! If this is what compassion looks like, heaven save us from it.

In 2009, when health care reform was in the air but before the passage of the Patient Protection and Affordable Care Act (what became known as Obamacare), business executive David Goldhill wrote a provocative article in the *Atlantic* magazine.[5] Goldhill had lost his father to an infection acquired at a hospital in New York City. Goldhill's experience and subsequent investigation alerted him to major problems in American health care, problems that persisted amidst enormous financial and technological riches. In the essay he underscored this paradox through a series of pointed questions:

> How can a facility featuring state-of-the-art diagnostic equipment use less-sophisticated information technology than my local sushi bar? How can the ICU stress the importance of sterility when its trash is picked up once daily, and only after flowing onto the floor of a patient's room? Considering the importance of a patient's frame of mind to recovery, why are the rooms so cheerless and uncomfortable? In whose interest is the bizarre scheduling of hospital shifts, so that a five-week stay brings an endless string of new personnel assigned to a patient's care? Why, in other words, has this technologically advanced hospital missed out on the revolution in quality control and customer service that has swept all other consumer-facing industries in the past two generations?

But Goldhill—a Democrat and, as he said, "long concerned about America's lack of a health safety net"—did not propose more robust government involvement. The problem with the current system, he recognized, had to do with the structuring of incentives, and a government takeover would only exacerbate it. The details of Goldhill's proposed solution are fascinating and moving, but not essential to delve into here. What is important is that he got the big thing right: "A guiding principle of any reform should be to put the consumer, not the insurer or the government, at the center of the system."

The Secret to Slashing Costs

Consumers selecting among various products, tapping into savings if necessary, choosing the services they determine best fit their needs; vendors working hard to gain and keep business, innovating to better serve customer needs, striving to provide personal and appealing service—this is the way virtually every other critical sector of the economy works. Why not health care?

Yes, health care is important and at times justifies major spending. Some increases in health care costs over the previous century are a function of new but expensive technologies providing valuable services that simply didn't exist in the past. A person rushed to the hospital with fatally blocked arteries may pay more for the health care he receives than he would have a hundred years ago, even adjusted for inflation. But in the early twentieth century the patient would simply have died, while today's patient will be rushed into the operating room and saved by open heart surgery. He may have just been given an extra ten or fifteen years of life. Most people would readily exchange a couple of new cars and houseboat for that. Health care is a field that has succeeded in creating valuable new services, services people are willing to pay for. That's one driver of increased costs, and we shouldn't forget it.

That said, it's not the only cost driver, and probably not even the primary driver. We have already looked at medical services that haven't been distorted by government interventions, such as LASIK surgery. When such a new technology appears, it's expensive at first. But gradually the price comes down as various competitors race to improve the technology and more and more physicians master the skill of providing the new service. It's the same pattern we see in other consumer services and products. What is a luxury one day—out of reach except to the wealthiest—in a relatively short time becomes a routine procedure for average patients.

When DVD players were first introduced into the market they were rather expensive. With market penetration still minimal, there weren't many manufacturers yet, and they were not mass produced. Economies of scale had not yet kicked in. But as the market for DVDs increased, the price for a player came down, and as that happened, more and more people were able to afford one. This led to still greater economies of scale and still lower prices. In 1999, 7 percent of American homes possessed DVD players; by 2006, it was 81 percent, and household penetration exceeded that of the previous cutting-edge technology, the VCR.[6] As of early 2012, a person could buy a Sony DVD player for about $30.

In effect wealthy people, who were among the first to buy DVD players, subsidized DVD player development for the rest of us. The same pattern is then repeated with the subsequent invention—Blu-ray, or whatever technology will ultimately replace the classic DVD. Although for the reasons outlined above we are less familiar with the costs of medical tests and procedures, the same price decreases can happen—and do—when the market is permitted to work.

When price increases appear to be out of control and there is no disaster to explain the upward-rushing costs, one may reasonably conclude that free competition in the market is being hampered. Why is the market in health care so dysfunctional? Because there is a separation of the one who pays and the one who uses the services. If these two were the same person, as in most of our purchases, there would be powerful incentives to lower prices and improve service. The most extreme cases are Medicare and Medicaid, where the person may have paid very little, or a very long time ago, or not at all for the government medical insurance. But a similar dynamic is at work with most private insurance plans, as they are now generally configured and delivered. The point cannot be overemphasized: the main source of health care payment is insurance plans with low copayments and low deductibles, purchased by employers so that the patient is shielded from the actual cost of a particular service. No incentive exists to inquire about pricing, let alone to shop around. Imagine if you purchased clothes in that way.

The consumer is also protected from one of the consequences of dangerous lifestyle choices—the sometimes expensive cost of repairing the damage at the local clinic or hospital. This factor is not trivial. Four health behaviors—smoking, diet, physical inactivity, and alcohol use—account for 38 percent of all United States deaths.[7] Two-thirds of Americans are overweight, adding significantly to their risks of chronic diseases including Type 2 diabetes, heart disease, and cancer.[8] Twenty percent of adults are smokers.[9] The health benefits of balanced diet and exercise are well known. All of these behavioral components of health are largely controllable by individuals. Yet the incentive to make good choices and avoid bad ones is diluted by a third-party payer health care system.

And with the government being the largest (and growing) source of health care payments, there is also little or no incentive on the part of health care professionals to make pricing rational, to cut costs, or to improve quality.

All of this is on top of the competition-reducing regulations that act as barriers to entry for health care professionals. The American Medical Association (really a guild) helps limit the numbers of trained and licensed doctors; the FDA enforces draconian controls on the development of new drugs; and a plethora of laws forbid interstate insurance competition and require policyholders to pay for treatments that they never intend to use (and, in some cases, have moral objections to).

What confuses a lot of people is that they assume the U.S. health care system is "the capitalist approach" and then blame its ills on the free market. This appears to be filmmaker Michael Moore's assumption. But health care in the United States is far from a free market, and it is far from driven by the individual consumer of health care services. Thanks to a growing series of government interventions in the marketplace over the past several decades, our health care system now revolves around insurance companies, employers, hospitals, pharmaceutical companies, and government. This is the central problem.

President Obama's strategies for reforming the system will not improve the system—not under this or any other administration. By centralizing more power and responsibility in Washington, Obamacare pushes the individual even further away from medical decisions and costs. Government control over health care does not just limit the freedom of your doctor to do what he thinks is best for your health. It does not just constrain your health care choices. It does not just limit innovation by removing incentives for research and development. It covers the entire health care system in the suffocating blanket of a soulless bureaucracy. It may be instituted in the name of helping the poor. It may be instituted with the sincere intention of helping the poor. But in its actual effects, government health care is anything but compassionate.

The Right to Health Care Understood Aright

Some theologians and philosophers have spoken of a "right to health care." How are we to understand this? The issue is complex enough that Acton issued a monograph on the subject that I would recommend to anyone wishing to dig more deeply into this matter.[10] Here let me just call attention to two misguided, yet nearly ubiquitous assumptions about the right to health care. The first is that it means a right to every single desirable product and service that might be available. The second false assumption is that the government should be the primary or even the exclusive means of fulfilling that right.

Since human beings are made in the image of God, society does have certain obligations to offer basic care, love, and attention—including medical care. Human beings are owed certain things simply by virtue of being human. At the same time, no reasonable person would argue that the right to health care means a limitless right to goods and services—a right, in other words, to demand the limitless efforts of others to serve one's health care needs without remuneration of any kind. So while we can speak of a generalized "right to health care" (especially in the sense that people have a right not to have their health and life unreasonably endangered by others), that doesn't mean that the state should simply try and guarantee health care for everyone. The principle of subsidarity, mentioned in the previous chapter, indicates to us that when it comes to positive rights, other organizations and communities have a major responsibility to provide the necessary care before the state gets involved.

The Religious History of Health Care

The hard cases arise when people, through no fault of their own, simply run out of resources and still find themselves in grave need. For them, the religious community stands, as it has always stood, in a posture of solidarity and mercy. The resource of first resort must be those closest to the need, as we discussed in Chapter Seven. Here the principle of subsidiarity applies, calling people to act as neighbors to those closest to them who are in need. If the poor and marginalized are not to be neglected, there is no substitute for a vibrant sector of private, charitable, and typically religious institutions who can fill their needs.

It should come as no surprise, then, that religious communities are in the middle of the recent debate over health care. Catholic health care institutions treat one of every six patients in the United States. Catholic hospitals admit more than 5 million patients a year. Hundreds of other hospitals, clinics, and other care facilities were founded by or are managed by Jewish, Lutheran, Methodist, Adventist, and other Christian bodies.

Why is this? The short answer is that Christendom invented the hospital. I don't mean that Christianity invented the practice of trying to heal sick people. That effort is older than history. But Christianity brought a new urgency to the care of the sick. The teachings of Jesus made health care more than a means of employment, more even than a civic duty. He took service to the vulnerable to a deeper and more profound level when he told his followers that "as you did it to one of the least of these my brethren, you did it to me."

Two factors combined in Christianity to beget a revolution in the care of the sick. The first was this view of mercy to the vulnerable as in some mysterious way an encounter with Christ himself. This meant that care for the sick had to be personal. The second was that Christians were called in charity to lay down their lives for others. So they were willing to go to great lengths to provide care—even to risk losing their own lives, if necessary.

This radical commitment to serve the sick was demonstrated in the course of two plagues that struck the Roman Empire in the second and third centuries. While most pagans fled the cities, many Christians stayed behind to tend the sick and dying. In *The Rise of Christianity*, Baylor University sociologist Rodney Stark suggests that Christians were prompted to stay by the bedsides of dying patients and risk infection because of their great hope in the afterlife and their profound belief that to serve the sick was to serve their Master.

The second of these two great epidemics—called the Plague of Cyprian, after an early Christian saint who described it in his writings—struck in the year 250 and eventually claimed millions of lives throughout the empire. Alexandria alone lost some two-thirds of its population. The bishop of that city describes a pattern of behavior that would eventually transform how Christendom responded to the sick and dying:

> Most of our brother Christians showed unbounded love and loyalty, never sparing themselves, and thinking only of one another. Heedless of danger, they took charge of the sick, attending to their every need and ministering to them in Christ, and with them departed this life serenely happy; for they were infected by others with the disease, drawing on themselves the sickness of their neighbors and cheerfully accepting their pains. Many, in nursing and curing others, transferred their death to themselves and died in their stead.... The best of our brothers lost their lives in this manner, a number of presbyters, deacons, and laymen winning high commendation so that death in this form, the result of great piety and strong faith, seems in every way the equal of martyrdom.[11]

This description is illustrative of a pattern that would transform the West. As Guenter B. Risse explained in his Oxford University Press book on the history of hospitals, Christianity institutionalized "philanthropy and the creation of establishments to shelter and feed the poor, care for the sick, assist widows and the aged, and raise orphans."[12] What we today know as the hospital emerged under the inspiration of Christian mercy.[13]

Christianity's belief that God became incarnate as a human being galvanized the Christian community's commitment not merely to almsgiving and a spirit of generosity, but to an institution-building mission of mercy that resulted in institutions such as hospitals, universities, and orphanages. Even today faith-based institutions are especially critical providers of care to marginalized populations of the poor and diseased. For example, a 2007 World Health Organization study estimated that between 30 and 70 percent of the health care infrastructure in Africa was at that time owned by religious organizations. In Zambia, faith-based groups furnished more than 30 percent of all care and treatment services for AIDS patients; in Lesotho the figure was 40 percent.[14] Where religious and other non-governmental institutions that provide health care thrive, the poor can receive care while the government remains in the background, providing services relatively infrequently and only as a last resort.

Because of the vital role of Christianity in the history of health care, we should feel the gravity of what has been happening to religious hospitals and clinics in the past several decades—and in an accelerated fashion in the past few years. Government's increasing role in health care has tended to secularize these otherwise vibrant civil institutions—altering their meaning, culture, and mission, and compromising their effectiveness. As government reaches ever deeper into the health care sector, it forces these religious institutions to become more and more like secular institutions, until it actually begins to exclude people of conscience from remaining involved with the very institutions they created in the first place! This may strike some as merely a parochially Christian concern, but what's at stake is relevant to everyone in this country: both religious liberty and the recovery and maintenance of vibrant, loving, and authentic health care in America.

The principles we have discussed have some clear policy implications. In the last analysis, Obamacare leaves in place and actually expands the very structures that produced the health care crisis in the first place. If we are going to truly reform the way we provide for the sick in our society, we need to reconnect physician with patient, patient with payment, and all of them back to the rich moral and spiritual tradition that gave birth to hospitals in the first place.

Thoughtful people can disagree about the practical details, but we mustn't lose sight of the principles. If real progress toward genuinely universal and humane health care is to be made, the free and virtuous market must once again extend to our system of health care.

A genuine civil society and free market-based reform of our health care system will mean reform of the tax structure so as to encourage individual insurance and health care purchases rather than employer purchase (the fact that so many of us get health care through our employers is actually a creation of the federal tax code). It will also mean eliminating barriers to competition by, for example, permitting insurance providers to sell insurance policies across state lines and removing regulations that burden charitable providers to low-income people. And it will mean tort reform and, in turn, reform of our malpractice laws, since these raise costs by driving physicians to practice wasteful defensive medicine (for example, overprescribing medicines and diagnostic tests) to protect themselves against frivolous lawsuits.

While some kind of basic safety net is needed, we must find a way for decisions on medical care to be placed in the hands of patients and medical professionals, not bureaucrats. We must design incentives to decrease costs rather than increase them. For example we must dismantle the current regime under which Medicaid rewards states for recruiting more enrollees—and thus the incentive is to spend money, not to save it. Shouldn't we, instead, be seeking ways to *remove* people from dependence on government medicine—not by "kicking them to the curb" but by encouraging those who can to shoulder responsibility for their own health, and thereby retain the dignity and self-direction that comes with that responsibility? Trapping people in dependency isn't compassionate any more than paternalism constitutes good parenting. It's time for us to move toward a system that encourages human capacity and human flourishing.

Reform is also essential at the moral level. The medical community is surely not immune to the moral erosion of our culture, with its "looking out for number one" mentality, particularly when doctors have been distanced from patients by bureaucracy.

Under the influence of these twin forces—bureaucratic expansion and moral decline—the health care industry increasingly has taken to viewing patients as government-funded piggy banks, to be tapped for money by any means available—sometimes legally, sometimes not (witness the monstrous problem of Medicare and Medicaid fraud).

Fortunately, there are still armies of compassionate and ethical doctors, nurses, and therapists who know how to make a good living while remaining fully human, but they are under pressure from increasing disincentives to carry out their work in an ethical and patient-centered manner. As effective a tool as the market is for allocating resources, we cannot yield to the seduction that the power of economic freedom can in itself generate a system of health care marked by honesty and love. Freedom is necessary, but never sufficient. We must re-connect health care with the moral inspiration that animated it historically.

As part of my ministry I have worked in many different hospital settings, from ministering to some of the first AIDS patients undergoing experimental drugs in the 1980s to being present with patients in pediatric oncology. I have been with numerous families as they finally, and with great difficulty, let their loved ones slip into eternity. I will never forget the long night spent keeping vigil with the family of a seven-year-old girl as she was finally removed from a respirator. I held her mother's hand as we watched her beautiful daughter draw her last breath. Not all of the economic freedom in the world, not all the personal liberty in the world, not all the money in the world, could have given those patients and their families the thing they most needed in those sacred moments.

When I visit the sick of my parish today, I know that what they seek is meaning in their suffering, to be heard without presuppositions, to be loved, and to have their dignity respected. I have seen doctors and nurses who bring that intangible something-more to the medical care they provide, something that transcends their technical expertise. Because each of their patients is so much more than biological, the acknowledgment of the spiritual is, I believe, imperative for a completely curative environment, or at least for a peaceful acquiescence to the summons of eternity. I see the difference it makes with the patients, both physically and spiritually. I have also witnessed patients cared for by doctors and nurses who, while technically proficient, have nonetheless succumbed to that insidious spirit that would instrumentalize human relationships. In such cases, I have seen the "care"—however technically proficient—withering the spirits of their patients.

Modern health care institutions originated in Christian charity. To my mind this fact demonstrates the intrinsic connection between health care and service motivated by love. Health care that reflects the value of the human person is the best health care.

The more our society politicizes health care, even in the name of the common good, the more we will weaken this critical tie. The very institutions in which mercy became flesh will be marginalized, as a cold secularist ideology achieves a monopoly on medical services. This challenge requires of us purpose and clarity of thought in the political arena, but it requires more than this. Deep reform will require the Christian community to once again seek out the vulnerable and in them to re-discover Christ, the final source of healing and redemption, the balm of Gilead. This is health care reform of a kind undreamt by any political party.

Suggestions for Further Reading

Michael F. Cannon and Michael D. Tanner, *Healthy Competition: What's Holding Back Health Care and How to Free It* (Cato Institute, 2007).

Donald P. Condit, *A Prescription for Health Care Reform* (Acton Institute, 2009).

The Galen Institute website at www.galen.org.

David Goldhill, "How American Health Care Killed My Father," *Atlantic*, September 2009, http://www.theatlantic.com/magazine/archive/2009/09/how-american-health-care-killed-my-father/7617/.

Health Care in America: A Catholic Proposal for Renewal (Catholic Medical Association, 2004), http://www.cathmed.org/assets/files/CMA%20Healthcare%20Task%20Force%20Statement%209.04%20Website.pdf.

CHAPTER 9

Caring for the Environment Doesn't Have to Mean Big Government

Q: Don't competition and profit-making inevitably exploit the environment?

■ ■ ■

A: Economic freedom isn't the enemy of conservation. It's an ally. Nor are human beings necessarily a threat to the well-being of the planet. An ownership society is a stewardship society where human creativity that holds the key to meeting environmental challenges is encouraged. Many environmental problems can be traced to ill-defined or poorly enforced property rights. One of the best ways that governments can help the environment is by clearly defining and protecting those rights.

■ ■ ■

Increasingly in the last twenty years, concern for the environment has manifested itself in the religious community in various ways, some more and some less thoughtful. A few years ago I debated Matthew Fox, a former Catholic priest who had left traditional Christianity behind to found what can fairly be called a new religion based on "creation spirituality." There were a number of telling points in our exchange, but I remember two most vividly. First, Fox drew a parallel between the practice of clearcutting in America's forests and the Nazi Holocaust. Second, when I pressed him about whether there was a hierarchy in the natural world—that is, whether human beings possessed some rights that were more important than or additional to the rights of natural objects such as trees and rocks, he could not bring himself to concede the point. In his view there was no essential difference between a slug and a human person.

We can all agree that environmental abuses—such as the indiscriminate clearcutting of forests with no concern for the future—are harmful. But to draw a moral equivalence between the demise of a stand of pines and the incineration of millions of Jews is to cross a dangerous line. Fox is an extreme case, but I fear that the basic errors that underpin his worldview are becoming increasingly common.

To answer those errors, expertise in climatology, zoology, or biology is not enough. Theology, ethics, and philosophy come into play as well. The scientific and policy details of the environmentalism debate—air and water pollution, climate change, genetically modified organisms, species protection—aren't the focus of the present book. My hope in this chapter is to bring a deeper understanding of how theologically informed economic actors might approach this hotly debated and complex topic.

Despite its complexity, one thing about the environmental debate is obvious: it is too often a clash of extremes. On the one hand you have people who view nature as one giant dumping ground, as a resource to rape and discard. At the other extreme are those like Matthew Fox, who virtually worship nature or view human beings as a disease. The sound Christian view is neither to worship nature nor to despise it. In the biblical understanding, nature is God's creation, pronounced good by its Creator, and human beings have been made stewards of it. This view is not only better for human liberty; it's also better for the environment.

Christianity Caricatured

Unfortunately, the orthodox Christian doctrine of creation stewardship often gets lost in all of the extremist rhetoric and straw man attacks. Though you won't learn it from listening to the proponents of "eco-theology," Christianity is incompatible with the belief that man is intractably in conflict with nature, and that we're supposed to root for him to lose. Some radicals have gone so far as to say the earth would be best off if the human population were all but wiped out, or at least vastly reduced, by a plague.[1] Meanwhile, they seem to have a remarkable ability to ignore the cruelty of "nature red in tooth and claw"[2] when unhindered by the presence of man.

In 1967, Lynn White (1907–1987), professor of medieval history and environmentalist, touched off a controversy when he published what came to be a hallowed article in the annals of the environmental movement in the prestigious journal *Science*: "The Historical Roots of Our Ecologic Crisis."[3] In that essay White characterized the spread of Christianity as the root cause of the "crisis" he saw in the environment. He blamed Christian "dualism"—the purported Christian teaching that human beings are supposed to exploit nature. But White's characterization of the Christian understanding of creation—influential and foundational to contemporary environmentalism as it is—was and remains a grave distortion of what Christians actually believe.

White correctly observed, "What people do about their ecology depends on what they think about themselves in relation to things around them." Yes, as we have seen again and again throughout this book, our anthropology—our understanding of man—absolutely does shape how we act. White's mistake was in identifying the Christian worldview as a threat to nature.

If by "nature" White means creation, then Biblical religion is manifestly not dualistic, as he adamantly and repeatedly claims. In the Bible man is depicted as part of creation—though his place is at its apex—*and* as its steward. Jews and Christians are not called to violate or pillage nature any more than a master gardener is called to thwart and suffocate the land he tends. The Bible views earth as a realm that human beings are called to tend as gardeners.[4] (It is actually the various forms of eco-religion, creation spirituality, and earth worship, not Christianity, that are guilty of a radical dualism—as we will see shortly.)

Professor White, in the same *Science* essay, said that Christianity is uniquely responsible for growing environmental problems, since "by destroying pagan animism, Christianity made it possible to exploit nature in a mood of indifference to the feelings of natural objects." In fact, White seemed to want to return to an animism—he saw the natural world as the source of all value, humanity as an alien intruder, and God—if he existed at all—as so immanent in nature that he ceased to be distinguishable from it. (Professor White actually invoked St. Francis, who is the patron saint of ecology because of the saint's great love for creation. But he may not have known that St. Francis is also the patron saint of merchants, who are responsible for caring for the earth's resources and turning them to productive use.)

In more recent times, Rupert Sheldrake has attacked the Judeo-Christian tradition for emphasizing the supremacy of man over Mother Earth; he explicitly calls for a new animism.

The Book of Genesis gives us neither the supposed dualism that White censures Christianity for nor the monistic worldview that he and his intellectual heirs seem to want to put in its place. In the Biblical account, God is the source of all values—the ultimate ground of the good, the true, and the beautiful. Human beings are *essentially* part of his created order; and by the virtue of their created nature and rationality, they are placed at the head of creation as God's vicars to act in his stead as stewards. Because they are God's stewards, their care for the earth is not supposed to be arbitrary or narrowly anthropocentric. Instead it is *theocentric*—the human role is as a viceroy whose duties are prescribed and proscribed by God.

But as wrong as White and Sheldrake are about both Christianity and nature, other "ecotheologians" have actually taught me to appreciate one thing about White's particular strain of environmentalism—at least he did not try to hijack Christianity for pagan purposes. White did understand that the traditional faith of the West regarded man as fulfilling a special role in creation. While these authors miss the positive implications of the doctrine of man made in the image of God, at least they aren't trying to co-opt Christianity for the purpose of placing man and mole on the same ontological plane.

Christianity insists on the special role of human beings in creation in two ways that the anti-Christian environmentalists reject. The first, as already noted, is the doctrine of the *imago Dei*, the teaching in Genesis that human beings are made in the image of God. The second is the doctrine of the Incarnation of Jesus Christ. Christianity teaches that in God's entrance into human history, the human person's nobility was confirmed by God's choice of the human form. It follows that to exalt non-human forms of life above rational souls explicitly challenges the Christian doctrine of the special sanctity of human life.

This should make crystal clear the opposition between Christianity, on one hand, and, on the other hand, a worldview and cultural agenda that value human life less than that of the lower animals. It should also set the stage for an open and honest debate between the two opposed views of the world and man—a debate that all of Christendom should welcome.

Unfortunately, ecotheologians muddy the waters by arguing that the two are compatible. Until relatively recently, the distinction between genuine Christian theology and environmental spirituality was well understood. But in the 1980s the line between Green ideology and Christian ethics began to blur. Calvin B. DeWitt, a University of Wisconsin professor of environmental studies, led the way. He founded the Au Sable Institute for Environmental Studies and proceeded to underwrite a series of conferences, leading to the publication of three influential volumes: *Tending the Garden: Essays on the Gospel and the Earth*; *The Environment and the Christian*; and *Missionary Earthkeeping*.[5] These books articulated a radical nature-centered theology, reinterpreted Gospel stories in enviro-political terms, and adopted the teachings, goals, and means of the radical Green movement as fitting for the evangelical community.

At the same time, secular politics was becoming ever Greener. The 1980s represented the coming of age of environmentalism, a time when a new political movement portrayed man's impact on nature as the great evil in the world and untrammeled Mother Earth as the good to be restored and preserved.

It was the dawning of a new Manichaeism—an ancient rival to Christianity—which postulated that the universe was divided between dark and light, the dark pertaining mainly to man's physical qualities and light to spirituality. The disciples of Mani, the founder of Manichaeism, believed that it is evil to alter nature. Their high priests would sit under trees and wait for the melons to drop so as not to cause the plants pain by picking them.

This is a strange theory indeed, one implying that the lives of animals and plants are as precious as human beings' and also that all forms of life are equipped with rational souls and thereby equally in need of evangelization. Manichaeism would not only reduce the status of human life to that of the animal kingdom; if widely adopted and put into practice, it would reduce actual human life to starvation because of its radical implications for economic systems. A world ruled by Manichaeism would mean the massive curbing of production, economic exchange, innovation—and thus eventually cause mass starvation and death. We know not just from Christian teaching but from all of history that man's survival and flourishing depend on exercising responsible dominion over creation, tilling and keeping earth's garden, owning property and transforming it to the betterment of the human condition

To deny the valuable role that thoughtful, creative stewardship of nature has played is delusional—a delusion even more absurd than the socialist idea that society's resources are better owned by the state than by individuals. For all the problems inherent in socialism, at least this much can be said for even the most maladjusted among the socialists—they sold their social reforms as a means for making *human beings* better off. None of them ever asked the world to abolish private property and destroy the free market in a play to exalt the rights of minks and mud worms at the expense of human well-being.

Now it's true that your average secular environmentalist believes he is also doing what's best for humanity, since the destruction of the ecosystem would be just as bad for humanity as it would be for the rest of the animal kingdom. But for many years now the bad theology—or maybe I should say the anti-theology—of the radical environmental movement has been leaching into mainstream environmental thinking, compromising the clear and traditional understanding of man as capable of fulfilling a positive, creative, and energetic role in nature as a steward of creation.

As it was increasingly obvious that these trends were undermining a sound understanding of man and creation, the Acton Institute brought together twenty-five theologians, economists, environmental scientists, clergy, and policy experts in West Cornwall, Connecticut, in October 1999 to discuss the problem and lay the intellectual groundwork for further inquiry and response. Out of this meeting was born the idea of composing an interfaith statement that would express common concerns, beliefs, and aspirations about environmental stewardship. Over the course of several months, an early draft was vetted by many of the nation's leading Jewish, Catholic, and Protestant minds, and a final version of the Cornwall Declaration on Environmental Stewardship was agreed upon on February 1, 2000. The Acton Institute, along with the Interfaith Council for Environmental Stewardship (a broad-based coalition of individuals and organizations committed to the principles espoused in the Cornwall Declaration), began distributing the declaration and promoting its principles within the religious community.

Since that time, Acton and the ICES have continued to promote a sound approach to the environment—taking seriously the moral responsibilities of stewardship, the findings of scientific research, and the insights of economics. These efforts are valuable not only in promoting genuine environmental stewardship. They are also important in preserving free societies, for the unseemly underbelly of environmentalist leftism is an all-out campaign against the foundations of Western civilization. If that sounds paranoid or overblown, read on.

Environmentalism as an Extension of Marxism

I was in Nicaragua immediately after the fall of communism there in 1990. On the day that the new president, Violeta Chamorro, was being inaugurated, I noticed some pro-Sandinista demonstrators across from our hotel with large signs and gigantic puppets. I went over to speak with them. They could see that I was a priest but did not know that I was there supporting their new president. We began to speak about the demise of the Sandinista revolution in Nicaragua and discussed how it had come to this. I asked what they were going to do now that the communist Sandinistas were out of power. One of these young comrades told me: "We are going back to the United States to get involved in the environmental movement."

The moment he said that, I saw the whole scenario. Although environmentalism was raising some legitimate concerns about the abuse of the natural world, I perceived that it could also be a continuation of the failed socialist revolution. The props and actors are different, but the plot is the same. Marx's idea is that society is rife with conflict and hostility, mainly between workers and capitalists. As the well-being of workers and capitalists alike improved under capitalism—and indeed, the lines between the two groups were blurred—that idea grew less and less viable. So the Marxist model has morphed into the belief in an intractable conflict between man and nature—which also, like the intractable conflict between workers and capitalists, just happens to require turning more and more power over to the state to protect the vulnerable against the evil machinations of capitalism. The Marxist taxonomy is quite resilient. The problem, of course, is that it represents a complete repudiation of the Jewish-Christian worldview—and completely fails to account for reality.

Marxism was going to do away with private ownership. On the contrary, it is right—and a great contributor to the flourishing of the human race and the good of the planet—that human beings exercise their stewardship responsibility on earth over nature through *ownership*. St. Augustine articulates an early Christian understanding of the difference between us and the other creatures: "When we hear it said, 'Thou shalt not kill,' we do not take it as referring to trees, for they have no sense, nor to irrational animals, because they have no fellowship with us. Hence it follows that the words, 'Thou shalt not kill' refer to the killing of a man."[6] Augustine directly rejected the idea that plants and animals have rights equal to those of people. He ridiculed the idea that killing animals is the same as murder. We acknowledge that not a sparrow falls to earth without God's knowledge. Yet we demand the *humane* treatment of animals, not because they have rights—*we must not be abusive to them because it debases us.* We must not treat animals as animals treat each other.

Just as there is a natural interdependence between the owner of productive property and the worker, so there is between man and nature. It is in our interest to have a clean environment, but the way to do this is to unleash creativity and human intelligence. When we over-regulate the market and thus obstruct the free flow of knowledge, we cause people to overuse things that are relatively scarce and to overproduce things that are not as needed or valued. This is the source of many environmental problems. Consider the environmental history of communist Europe—the Soviet Union and its satellites had a truly atrocious record of stewardship of natural resources.

Professor White did get several facts right in that seminal essay—among them, that Christianity played a crucial role in sparking the scientific revolution. That great leap ahead in technology and living standards came about because Christianity views man as the creative steward of a rational creation, a creation that we can explore and understand because we are made in the image of the rational God who formed the cosmos. Copernicus—a Catholic cleric—reflected something of the mindset of many of the founders of modern astronomy when he wrote about searching out "the mechanism of the universe, wrought for us by a supremely good and orderly creator."[7]

This understanding of God, man, and creation, and the scientific revolution it helped to germinate has blessed the human race in countless ways. Though White largely ignores the positive side of this revolution, he is correct to say that the scientific revolution gave humanity new powers over its environment. One need not be a partisan of any ideology to recognize that this newfound power can be used for good or ill. The question then becomes what kind of political order functions best to channel the power and energy of science and human endeavor toward environmentally positive activity and away from what is destructive? Despite what the Marxist protesters I met in Nicaragua may have thought as they packed their duffle bags to go join the environmental movement in the

United States, it isn't socialism. In fact, it's precisely those systems that fail to defend private property rights that are most inclined to abuse the earth. There's a name for this in economics—"the tragedy of the commons." Private property is the best preserver of creation, and no greater environmental spoilage has been witnessed than in the old socialist Eastern bloc countries, where private property was abolished. Indeed, the communist regime in China has also had a horrendous track record on environmental protection.

The market economy, in contrast, is a forward-looking system of economic organization in which the scarcities of the future are imputed back into today's prices, which thereby signal the proper uses of resources today. If there's a scarcity of some resource looming on the horizon, prices will rise, telling people to shift consumption in a more affordable direction, while simultaneously attracting would-be entrepreneurs to see if they can discover or create more of the scarce resource in order to sell it at the rising price. We absolutely do have a duty to future generations, but that duty is more easily fulfilled by a system of rationing driven by price signals in a free economy than by bureaucratic edicts. The United States overbuilt houses in the previous decade, and China is now in the middle of a massive overbuilding campaign. Both resource-wasting housing booms were driven not by price signals in a capitalist economy but government financial engineering aimed at "stimulating the economy" and, in the process, disrupting and distorting the information built into prices in a free economy.

Political and economic freedom leads to an ownership society, as opposed to a rental society—and also as opposed to the kind of pseudo-ownership society created by the "liar loans" and other abuses that emerged during the government-inspired housing bubble. Real private ownership carries with it a different set of incentives from the incentives that arise from any other way of managing property. We can see this in the example of America's national forests. Although the general public assumes that the US Forest Service acts with the best interests of the environment in mind, the reality is far different. The incentive for forestry personnel is to maximize their budget, not to protect forests or even to maximize general revenue. Thus there is a greater emphasis on lumber harvests than would be expected under either an environmental ethic or a profit motive, because lumber harvesting means road building, and road building means big budgets for the Forest Service and lots of work for its employees—even though the service usually loses money on its timber harvest operations. In essence, timber companies' cutting of trees in our national forests is subsidized by taxpayers.[8] No private owner would tolerate such waste.

An additional and significant environmental advantage of preserving the freedom of the market economy is its capacity to generate wealth, which in turn gives society the latitude to take care of the commons such as rivers and lakes in ways that are not possible in more desperate circumstances. In most cases it will be very difficult to get people in extreme poverty stirred up about the health of the river downstream from them. And rightly so—in impoverished areas, most people are just trying to survive. This is why efforts to protect the environment that jeopardize economic progress should be viewed with skepticism. If we foster the conditions of economic development, and have a consistently high regard for private property, environmental sensitivity will come. When the basic needs of human beings are met, a growing care for our natural surroundings follows, particularly in an ownership society.[9]

Humanophobia

One of the chief concerns reiterated by environmental activists over the last three decades is resource depletion as a result of "overpopulation." This fear exacerbates the problem of what we can call humanophobia—that is, viewing human beings as a scourge on the planet. The logic of this concern is straightforward but ultimately misleading: The earth is finite in size. If the population keeps growing, eventually people will use up all of the resources.

The argument appears obvious, and yet it has been the basis for one false doomsday prediction after another. The following are but a few of the multitude that might be cited:

> When our coal mines are exhausted, the prosperity and glory of this flourishing and fortunate island are at an end. Our cities and great towns must then become ruinous heaps...and the future inhabitants of this island must live like its first inhabitants, by fishing and hunting.
>
> —John Williams, *Natural History of the Mineral Kingdom*, 1789[10]

> ...there is no probability that when our coal is used up any more powerful substitute will be forthcoming.
>
> —W. Stanley Jevons, *The Coal Question*, 1865[11]

> American oil supplies will run out in 13 years.
>
> —U.S. Department of the Interior, 1939[12]

> The world as we know it will likely be ruined before the year 2,000.... World food production cannot keep pace with the galloping growth of population.
>
> —The Environmental Fund, 1975[13]

> I would take even money that England will not exist in the year 2000.
>
> —Paul Ehrlich[14]

The last person mentioned here, Paul Ehrlich, has a history of imprudent wagering on such predictions. After all, his great claim to fame was his apocalyptic manifesto, *The Population Bomb* (1968), in which he asserted, "The battle to feed all of humanity is over. In the 1970's and 1980's hundreds of millions of people will starve to death in spite of any crash programs embarked upon now."[15] A decade later, Ehrlich (along with a friend of his, John Holdren—now Science and Technology advisor to President Obama) made a bet with the late Julian Simon. Simon contended that markets seek out alternatives and human beings find and create new resources, thus making better use of the earth's bounty and lowering the real price of commodities over time. He bet that the prices of any five metal commodities selected by his opponents would decrease. Ehrlich and Holdren, overlooking the role of human creativity or price signals in a free economy, bet that the prices were sure to rise. Simon won the bet.[16] Simon's successful bet underscores the experience of the human race with capitalism for hundreds of years: living standards gradually rise as human ingenuity and price signals create and orchestrate ever more effective ways to feed, clothe, and fuel society.

Beware the Zero-Sum Fallacy and Unintended Consequences

The resource depletion-overpopulation argument persistently generates false predictions for the simple reason that it is based on faulty premises. Its essential mistake is our old friend, the zero-sum fallacy. What is missing from Ehrlich's equation, what is so often missing in the entire environmental debate, is what we could call the "C" variable—creativity. Human beings create resources by discovering new uses for formerly bothersome things; the creativity of the human mind can even transform things that were previously considered deadly into life-enhancing medicines. One dramatic example is the breakthrough that came when scientists found a way to use the deadly toxin that causes botulism for an effective neurological treatment. Or take a more familiar example. Ordinary sand has been converted into a means for revolutionary communication twice over—silicon for computer chips and fiber optic cables for carrying telecommunication information far more efficiently than the more expensive copper cables they replaced. Oil is another example. For most of history it was little more than a mucky annoyance that bubbled up from the ground here and there—until human ingenuity harnessed it for use in the internal combustion engine.

One could fill a library with such examples.

It's also important to understand that when a natural resource does run short, it does not run out overnight. As its supply declines, it becomes more precious, and thus more costly. When this happens, a natural process of rationing emerges. The price rises and people begin to use the resource more judiciously. The higher price also inspires creative people to respond in a couple of ways. Some of them will search out new methods for stretching the resource, knowing that people would happily pay for such a thing given the rising price of the resource in question. Other creative people will search out and perfect substitutes. This has happened repeatedly over history and it is happening as you read this book, as automakers craft more efficient engines, energy innovators learn how to turn organic waste into electricity, and agricultural scientists continue to improve crop yields. All of these activities are orchestrated by the price function. There is no more efficient, natural, and elegant way to encourage real conservation and progress at the same time.

However—and this bears repeating—for prices to do their job, there must be a functional market and defined property rights. Where these institutions are not in place, what occurs is another instance of the tragedy of the commons. When nobody owns the resources in question but all are permitted to make use of them, people race to devour the resource in order to get as much as possible before it runs out. The incentive is to deplete rather than conserve. The plight of many endangered species can be understood in this way. When animals are hunted to the point of extinction, it is often because no one has ownership of—and therefore responsibility for—the animals in question.

Such was the case with the decimation of the American bison in the nineteenth century, and we can observe the same problem with species of concern today, such as tigers and elephants. This is why creative environmentalists recommend that such animals be made the property of local people in India and Africa. In this way, they would become an asset to be managed, protected, and increased, rather than a threat to be removed (as a danger to human life) or a common resource to be exploited (by poachers). The good news is progress is being made using precisely these strategies.[17]

Enlisting the power of markets, ownership, and human creativity in the cause of conservation works better to protect endangered species than using heavy-handed government regulation. One of the serious dangers of government intervention is the possibility of unintended consequences.

This danger was illustrated vividly in the fallout from the Endangered Species Act of 1973. The Act, intended to protect rare animals, had the effect of turning them into a liability for property owners whose lands they occupied—since the public discovery of one of these endangered animals on a farm or ranch meant that the property owner could now look forward to a host of complex rules about how he could and couldn't use his property. So what was the actual result of the well-intentioned new policy? Property owners tended to limit the appropriate habitat for the endangered species, further threatening their survival. The less scrupulous even practiced a strategy captured in the grimly memorable phrase "shoot, shovel, and shut up."[18]

The lesson is clear. Those who are quick to advocate government intervention on environmental matters need to carefully consider all of the potential consequences of their policies. This applies to everything from protection of endangered species to concerns about global warming. Histrionic calls to hand ever more power over to the government before the sky falls need to be resisted. Stewardship of creation involves patience, prudence and deliberation, not grandiose schemes thrown together in an atmosphere of hysteria. All too often hastily adopted measures may hasten the very disaster they are designed to prevent.

Ours is an astoundingly complex, diverse, and treasure-filled world, awaiting the decoding of its richness and resources for human betterment—which in turn means an earth that's a cleaner, more wholesome, and more prosperous home for all species. Ultimately nature is comprehensible, even if its greatness remains mysterious, because it was fashioned by a rational intelligence and entrusted to the rational human family which, in turn, is expected to be productive and prudent in its care. It is our great privilege to have this world in our care, and thus to be cooperators with God in its continual creation.

Suggestions for Further Reading

E. Calvin Beisner, *Where Garden Meets Wilderness: Evangelical Entry into the Environmental Debate* (Eerdmans, 1997).

Effective Stewardship DVD Curriculum (Acton Media, 2009). For more information see http://www.effectivestewardship.com/.

Environmental Stewardship in the Judeo-Christian Tradition, ed. Michael Barkey (Acton Institute, 2000).

Bjørn Lomborg, *The Skeptical Environmentalist: Measuring the Real State of the World* (Cambridge University Press, 2001).

Robert H. Nelson, *The New Holy Wars: Economic Religion Versus Environmental Religion in Contemporary America* (Penn State University Press, 2010).

Julian Simon, *The Ultimate Resource II* (Princeton University Press, 1998), available online at http://www.juliansimon.com/writings/Ultimate_Resource/.

CHAPTER 10

A Theology for Economic Man

Q: What does theology have to do with economics?

■ ■ ■

A: Economics at its most fundamental level is not about money; it is about human action. How we answer the big questions—Who am I? Why am I here? Where did I come from? Where am I going? What is man?—has an enormous impact on every facet of our lives, including how we work and buy and sell, and how we believe such activities should be directed—on economics, in other words.

■ ■ ■

He is the sort of creature you expect to meet in a dystopian science fiction novel: his outline seems human, but as you move closer, something appears to be off. It is not exactly that the shade of his skin is unnatural;

it is more that its texture is, well, un-textured. The creature is bloodless and cold to the touch. Everything is in place, yet somehow nothing fits. Who can this alien being who is so frequently placed before me for my consideration be? Even his name is foreign, exotic—*homo economicus*. He shares so many of the features of a real man that his outline is the same, but he is not fully human, not real.

Homo economicus is the theoretical construct that appears frequently in the work of mainstream economists. His name is Latin for *economic man*. He is self-interested. His sole purpose in life is to maximize utility. He never stops calculating costs and benefits, and he is anxious to render these in monetary terms so they can be put on a balance sheet and bought or sold in a market. The results dictate his next choices in life. This pattern repeats itself every day from maturity until death, and in every aspect of life.

Homo economicus serves a purpose in the economics literature—in the same way as a caricature, with its bold and exaggerated lines, brings into high relief a crucial feature that might otherwise go unnoticed. But we need to be careful not to mistake *homo economicus* for an accurate representation of man. In real life, people are motivated by much more than what economists describe as "maximizing utility"—especially where "utility" is understood in narrowly materialistic terms. The economic truth of economic man is true enough (you ignore human self-interest and the laws of supply and demand at your peril), but it is not the whole truth about who human beings are.

Any man who was only *economic man* would be a lost soul. And any civilization that produced only *homines economici* to fill its markets, courts, legislative bodies, and other institutions would soon enough be a lost civilization. Familial love, voluntary dedication to philanthropy and faith, the creation of art and music would be at their most minimal level, and whole sectors of life would completely vanish. Focusing the whole of life on the acquisition of quantifiable goods does not bring true happiness or peace, as almost everyone knows. We all have material appetites, but we do not (pray God) always feed them. Imagine if we did!

Fortunately people are also motivated by desires that go deeper than sensual gratification. Human beings find ultimate fulfillment not in acquisition but in developing, sharing, and using their God-given creative capacities for good and giving of themselves to others—for love. This, by the way, isn't merely the pie-in-the-sky thinking of a Catholic priest. There is hard data to back it up. Researchers have found that sudden, unearned wealth does not permanently alter one's level of happiness. What does tend to make people happier is earned success—in other words, the feeling of accomplishment that comes with a job well done, a job that others find valuable.[1] Failing to understand that man is more than *homo economicus* will lead to major errors in addressing social problems. If we treat only the symptoms of social ills—slapping more meddlesome regulation, government spending, or targeted tax cuts onto the surface of a problem without nourishing the wellsprings of human happiness—our solutions will fail.

Allow me to illustrate. Some years ago I moved into a home in Michigan that had a lovely wraparound porch in the front, with a large oak tree nearby to provide a delightful and refreshing shade. It was an enchanting place to sit and watch the world go by on a summer's evening, the perfect place for meandering conversations about art, theology, and literature with the men in my religious community and our visitors. I grew up in Brooklyn, so trees have always held a special fascination for me. (A tree did grow in Brooklyn once, but it died before I got over to see it.) I would sit on that serene porch and study the tree. It went up about four stories, towering over the house. I was curious about the fact that while half of it was in full foliage, the other half was desiccated—the leaves dead and falling off. It was about that time that I made a great discovery. This boy from Brooklyn found out that there is such a thing as a "tree doctor."

As I say, it was a rare enough miracle even to see a tree when I was growing up in Brooklyn. To learn now that there were physicians who specialized in treating them was quite intriguing. The tree doctor came and looked at the bark of our beautiful tree, picked off some pieces, and then bent down to examine the soil. He inspected the dead leaves and stood back and took in the tree as a whole. He then walked up to the porch with a face as grave as any brain surgeon emerging from the surgical theater with bad news. "If you had contacted me sooner, we might have been able to save the tree," he said, "But I'm afraid the disease has progressed too far." And then he pronounced his diagnosis: "The tree is dead."

Caught up in the emotion of the moment, I exclaimed, "But, doctor!"

Then I caught myself and remembered that we weren't talking about a close relative. I took a breath and adopted a more Socratic tone. "Listen. How can it be dead? It has leaves that are in full bloom! The majority of the branches are blooming. They're blossoming. How can it be dead?"

He said, "Well, that is an illusion. The sap is still working its way through the tree. A part of the tree will bloom, but progressively fewer and fewer leaves will blossom. The real and immediate danger is this massive tree is sitting right next to your house, and with the right storm and the right wind, it will come down on your house." He paused and then continued, "So you have to take the tree down."

Any time I think of that tree—now long gone—I cannot help but think about our society. For me, the analogy is inescapable, even if I still have high hopes. Something seems so very wrong with the world around us, as though it's infected with something exogenous—and here I refer to something over and above the perennial condition of broken humanity. The disease that we fight has already manifested itself in some dead leaves, and we shouldn't let the accompanying healthy appearances of the other leaves fool us. We are living off a legacy we did not achieve. And we need to address the underlying causes of this sickness before it overwhelms us.

If one ponders the state of our society carefully, one finds signs of human flourishing side by side with creeping desiccation. Our culture seems to have all the answers, but answers to all the wrong questions. We confuse facts with meaning, and imagine we can Google our way to wisdom. Like Marcellus in Shakespeare's *Hamlet*, we sense that "something is rotten in the state of Denmark," even if we have difficulty recognizing the ghost right in front of us, let alone the solution to the civilizational crisis that besets us. Could this be what the end of freedom looks like? One thing seems certain: something in our world is distracted, disordered, out of joint. We see it all around us and, if we are honest, we find it inside of ourselves as well.

So much of the current political and economic debate is like the man in Plato's cave, mistaking shadows for substance. Talking points are not a philosophy of life nor are they good governance. Strong currents are tugging at us, pulling us away from our moorings, pulling us away from a clear vision of a free and virtuous society—the one that the American Founders envisioned, and that we still hunger for. Their vision was anchored not in whether we cut our deficit 3 percent or 5 percent, increase border security 2 percent or 20 percent, extend this or that benefit. I am not saying that these particulars are unimportant. But to understand how to get things right, we must look at more fundamental questions—not "What should we *do*?" but "Who *are* we?" A right understanding of who we are, and how we relate to nature, one another, and God, can be the only solid basis for a society worthy of the human person.

Aristotle pointed out that a small error at an early stage leads to big problems later on. Because our political and cultural leaders have gotten the anthropology wrong, they have gotten freedom wrong, have gotten society wrong. They have neglected the very soil our ancestors cultivated, nourished, and used to grow the freest, most prosperous, ethical, and progressive political experiment in human history. It was never perfect, to be sure, and it contained some especially noxious weeds even at the beginning. Many of those sins have been rooted out. Our problem now is different. A disease is threatening the good roots themselves—the very ideas and institutions that formed the basis of this nation's remarkable success. The disease runs deep, and debating the latest "bill on the hill" in Washington will do nothing to change that fact.

That's the bad news. The good news is that by rolling up our sleeves and digging for the truth, by retrieving a right understanding of the human person, we can turn things around. The tradition that gave birth to a morally animated liberty—not merely the power to do what one *wants* but the right to do what one *ought* (as Lord Acton observed[2])—is not a tradition of mere utility, selfishness, pleasure-seeking, or determinism. Freedom rightly understood is not a license to behave like spoiled adolescents but rather the noble birthright of creatures made in the image of God. As long as we refuse to sell this birthright for a mess of materialist pottage, hope remains.

Vocation—Calling

Many people consider the phrase "the call of the entrepreneur" an oxymoron, like "the charity of the leech." But the Judeo-Christian ethic offers a positive view of the moral potential of business. In a figurative sense, God is the prime "entrepreneur," the model of all entrepreneurship, the Creator who is generous in his creativity. But people in general are suspicious of business. The unstated presupposition of even many business ethics programs is that there is something essentially wrong with enterprise—not that something has gone wrong in practice for one reason or another, but that there is something fundamentally impious about business itself. The marketplace is so suspect that an alien ethic must be imported to keep the Tasmanian devil of greed and exploitation in check. If business is by its very nature fundamentally dishonest and destructive, it makes sense to have political bureaucrats regulating it to within an inch of its life. That, of course, assumes that bureaucrats, public officials, and politicians—being free of the original sin of business—are immaculately conceived and not subject to temptations or prone to error.

A different paradigm of the economy is required if we are to understand the human person fully. Mother Teresa gave us a glimpse of how we ought to see economic issues when she—who was neither an economist nor a theologian—nonetheless demolished Marx's notion of the class struggle with a single comment. "We have no right to judge the rich," she said. "For our part, what we desire is not a class struggle but a class encounter, in which the rich save the poor and the poor save the rich."[3]

We are *more* than the caricature of *homo economicus*. We are *not* simply utility maximizers. The radical individualism assumed by so many secular economists is frankly a truncated picture of humanity. (I don't mean *rugged individualism* in the sense of a John Wayne character stepping up and saving the town rather than being a leech on the town. We call those brave men heroes, not radical individualists.) Some people do live self-serving and largely isolated lives of pleasure-seeking, using others to that selfish end. But if your political system is all about protecting and promoting this kind of lifestyle—at the expense of the civil institutions and culture that connect people in community, strengthening and enriching them—then your society will not remain for long either free or virtuous.

Let's return here to the prescient vision that Alexis de Tocqueville penned more than 170 years ago, foreseeing the way that freedom could end. He warned not of the despotism of a military dictator, but of a more insidious tyranny that he feared would take hold, as he put it, "in the very shadow of the sovereignty of this people." This was de Tocqueville's vision: "I see an innumerable crowd of men, all alike and equal," and above them "stands an immense and protective power which alone is responsible for looking after their enjoyments and watching over their destiny. It is absolute, meticulous, ordered, provident, and kindly disposed." This ruling power, de Tocqueville said, "spreads its arms over the whole of society, covering the surface of social life with a network of petty, complicated, detailed, and uniform rules" until it "reduces each nation to nothing more than a flock of timid and hardworking animals with the government as shepherd."[4] It all sounds too terribly familiar. Have we actually reached the state of tyranny that de Tocqueville foresaw? Is this the end of freedom?

To understand how we might still escape the end of freedom in that sense, it is necessary to investigate the end of freedom in another sense—*end* in the sense of aim or purpose. We may be tempted to think, initially, that freedom is its own purpose or end. But freedom, despite the natural human yearning for it, is not a goal or a virtue in itself. We have freedom *for* something. Once the millions living under the yoke of totalitarian domination in Central and Eastern Europe were freed from communist domination, they had to use their newfound liberty for *something*. Freedom is an instrumental goal. Once it is achieved, we naturally ask, "And then?" What is the answer to the "And then?" about freedom? Ultimately the aim of freedom must be the truth, and the Truth. What else would be worthy of filling the void?

This is why the role of religious institutions in addressing the current crisis in our society goes well beyond their instrumental value as social service providers. Only an anthropology—an understanding of man—rooted in the truth about his nature and his ultimate destiny can serve as the proper foundation for a flourishing society. Truth is freedom's goal—and also, as a practical matter, truth is the necessary guarantor of human freedom.

First, faith reminds people of the limits of material existence and of their final destination. And being reminded of our ultimate destination is essential for individuals in organizing our life together. Recognizing that heaven on earth is impossible, we do not pursue utopian schemes. But we also recognize that what we do here contains in it the seeds of eternity. These lines from one of the principal documents of the Second Vatican Council say it well: "While we are warned that it profits a man nothing if he gain the whole world and lose himself, the expectation of a new earth must not weaken but rather stimulate our concern for cultivating this one. For here grows the body of a new human family, a body which even now is able to give some kind of foreshadowing of the new age."[5]

The twentieth-century German Lutheran theologian and martyr Dietrich Bonhoeffer also speaks to this: "The Christian's field of activity is the world. It is here that Christians are to become engaged, are to work and be active, here that they are to do the will of God; and for that reason, Christians are not resigned pessimists, but are those who while admittedly not expecting much from the world are for that very reason already joyous and cheerful in the world, for that world is the seedbed of eternity."[6]

It is no coincidence that Christian civilization was one of the first societies to create a broad middle class, a class that grew up out of the artisans and merchants and craftsmen that aristocrats tend to disdain, the kind of people who in all previous civilizations were never allowed to thrive and flourish beyond a certain level in any great number. It's no coincidence because the doctrine of the Incarnation taught European men and women that the Creator had sent his Son to become flesh and blood, to work as a humble carpenter here on this earth. The pagan aristocratic disdain for the earthy and the mundane could still get a foothold in the sinful human heart, but with Christianity, it no longer had a theological foothold.

Judaism and then Christianity taught men and women that ordinary physical labor is dignified and worth seeking to further dignify, that there is nothing suspect or unworthy in it. This view has the power to interpenetrate every level of a society and transform the way people approach all kinds of occupations. I'm reminded of a story I heard about a young man who entered a monastery. When the fellow was finally allowed to do so, he wrote to his family expressing his joy of discovering his vocation. He told his father a little about the life inside the walls of the monastery and how all the monks would rise from their beds in the middle of the night to return to the chapel. There, "when the entire world is hushed," as the young monk put it, they would pray for the world, the solemn voices of the monks chanting psalms that resonated through the chapel's stone walls. It was in this moving experience, he explained to his father, that he had discovered his vocation.

His father, who was a very devout and wise man, wrote this back to his son: "Dear Son, your mother and I are overjoyed to hear how you are adjusting to your vocation and your new life inside the walls of the monastery, and please know that we will pray for you now as we always have prayed for you. There is only one thing I ask you to keep in mind, my son, as you grow in the knowledge of your vocation and that is this: many a night, 'when all the world was hushed,' your mother and I rose from our beds to change your dirty diapers. And in doing this we found our vocation."

To be able to find God's call in the mess of a baby's dirty diapers is, surprising as it may seem, a reiteration of the message of the Incarnation of Christ: The eternal, ineffable God was born into the world and placed in a manger, a feed trough for animals. He became flesh and dwelt among us because he wants to be known concretely, personally, and intimately by his creatures. He is Emmanuel, "God with us," in our work and play, on the floors of our stock exchanges and in our butcher shops—he is in even these places, or there is no Emmanuel. The Incarnation demonstrates God's love for us, yes, absolutely. But it also reinforces the idea that this world, fashioned by God and pronounced "good" by him has purpose beyond its physicality. It is "charged with the grandeur of God," as the Jesuit poet Gerard Manley Hopkins put it—and not merely in the dazzling-sunrise-from-a-mountaintop sense but "like shining from shook foil." In other words, it is so charged with his grandeur that, if we had but eyes for it, we would find God's glory breaking out in the most ordinary of things and circumstances. We would understand that the offer of his grace can be discovered anywhere and at any time in the whole of the universe.

So the physical is itself a kind of catechism of God's offer of love. If we creatively touch it anywhere, probing it and seeking to grasp its true meaning deep down, each of us can discover its Author as well. I am convinced that the pursuit of excellence sincerely undertaken, in even the most humble of legitimate occupations, is a way to encounter the whole truth of the universe—an inchoate search for God. "Sacred" and "temporal" do not describe a radical separation, but instead a relationship between two interpenetrating realities—the "dust of the ground" and "the breath of life" from which God formed humankind (Genesis 2:7).

The Truth revealed in the Incarnation can also inoculate us from the growing moral relativism of our culture. Those who claim that right and wrong have no stable meaning promise to liberate us from old structures, but in reality relativism undermines the rule of law and invites tyranny. Princeton professor Robert George has noted that people who imagine that relativism is the best guarantor of tolerance and freedom of belief couldn't be more wrong. If everything is relative in matters of morality, how can one make the case against a Stalin or Hitler? Without moral absolutes, would we be able to speak of universal human rights, or denounce female genital mutilation or child sacrifice, incest or rape? A firm belief in a transcendent moral order is the only guarantee of the "unalienable rights" of all people.

This is exactly what ancient Athens lacked when Socrates tried to defend himself against the mob. Perhaps because of the Greek religion—the Olympian gods who were largely amoral or even immoral (raping, bickering, cheating, and so forth)—Socrates was unable to make an effective appeal to any higher law, and so the great Athenian democracy descended into mob rule. Of course Christian societies can also descend into mob violence, but they must first dispense with what their own theological understanding tells them about human beings and their dignity and rights. Incarnational theology has served and can continue to serve as a bulwark protecting the legitimate rights of minorities. It is no coincidence that Christian civilization was the first to achieve widespread toleration for people of different races and religions.

The theological truth that human beings have the capacity for virtue and greatness has played a crucial role in the birth of freedom in the West. So too has the truth that humans are fallen and sinful. The doctrine of original sin is not an attack on human dignity, but actually a crucial support. The recognition of our limitations, and even of our capacity to betray our highest values—an existential truth about the human condition that G. K. Chesterton quipped was "the only part of Christian theology which can really be proved"[7]—enables us to face squarely the all-too-real effects of that primordial sin.

An understanding of human sinfulness makes us appropriately modest in our plans—we do not assume selfless love in others, but acknowledge self-interest. And so, as James Madison insisted, we build nations fit for men, not angels.[8] The doctrine of original sin does not permit us to imagine that there is a group of pre-fallen mandarins to whom we can entrust unchecked political power, people so wise and so good that we need not divide and disperse power in a subsidiary fashion. The atheistic and neopagan political ideologies of the previous century (communism and Nazism, both variants of socialism) lacked this notion of fallenness and the modesty that it requires of us, and quickly produced totalitarian regimes for lack of a proper fear of unchecked political power.

Finally, sound theology continually reminds us of the right understanding of human equality, which is not an excuse for class warfare or for material leveling. Instead, it posits inherent human dignity and worth and equality of rights—the basis for the bond of solidarity we share by virtue of our common origin and transcendent purpose, which drives us to care for the vulnerable, even at personal risk and sacrifice.

The Dead

To imagine that theology—or if you prefer, a right understanding of the human person—doesn't matter is to forget the most cataclysmic features of the twentieth century—Hitler and Stalin and Mao and Pol Pot, not to mention the eugenics movement of the early twentieth-century United States.

My brother watched the events of September 11, 2001, from the roof of his Brooklyn home. He later told me that the ashes of those murdered that autumn morning fell across every borough of New York—ashes like the snowflakes at the close of James Joyce's story, "The Dead," falling all across a city I know so well, with whose people and accents I am so well acquainted. After my brother related this to me, I had an image in my mind of those ashes settling on the lake at Prospect Park where I used to go fishing, softly descending on Coney Island, on the beach where I first learned to swim, and encircling the bell tower of Regina Pacis where I celebrated my first Mass as a priest, wafting on to Old Calvary cemetery where my father was buried and later my mother. I see the ashes that bright and sparkling late-summer morning making their descent on the whole of the city, the ashes of corporate executives, secretaries, and janitors, of firefighters from Brooklyn and Queens, men who lived in neighborhoods just like my own, firefighters like Stanley Smagala, whose wife Dena was pregnant with their daughter Alexa when the Towers fell.

I know the sort, their down-to-earth qualities and rough virtues of courage and hard work. I believe I may also now know something about the ideology employed by the man who orchestrated the attacks. In many people's minds, Osama bin Laden was simply a holdover from a primitive form of Islam. But if you listen closely to some of the man's own recorded messages to the world, a more complex portrait emerges. In what may have been his last recorded video message, released after he had been killed and just after the tenth anniversary of the September 11 attack, bin Laden said that "the path to stop the hegemony of capitalism is to carry out a real radical change" so that President Obama "will be liberated, and with him, everyone else, from the hegemony of these corporations."

Whether bin Laden's political ideology was deeply influenced by socialist thinking is an open question. What is undeniable is that bin Laden found it useful to tap into socialism's anti-capitalist mentality and class-warfare vocabulary. With the fall of Soviet communism, many assumed that such thinking was in permanent retreat, but the impulse is never further away than human nature itself. It pipes a tune seductive to the darkest elements of the human heart—envy, sloth, pride—while promising speedy solutions to problems that the better angels of our nature crave to see remedied.

To build an authentically free and virtuous society is far more complicated and difficult, requiring habituation to just deeds, both visible and invisible. But as far as I have been able to discern in my circuitous odyssey from my childhood home in Brooklyn across America and the political spectrum, political, economic, and religious freedom is simply the best plan for human persons to seek and attain genuine goods. The free market rewards greatness and excellence instead of trying to eradicate them. It permits men and women the space to express, pursue, and create higher things. And it leaves room for the most effective kind of charity to those in need.

Freedom is indispensible to the flourishing of a virtuous society, and virtue is the indispensable glue to maintain and make sense of freedom, calling it to the higher end of truth. Without virtues—which are more than "values," because virtues are objective rather than a matter of subjective preference—we are susceptible to either of two temptations: to seek tyranny over others or to permit tyranny over ourselves, often because we idolize security and material comfort.

One would think that the connection between free markets and lives of virtue would be obvious in this "land of the free and home of the brave." But there are voices in our nation and world that dispute the connection, and do so in the name of religion and morality. Since co-founding the Acton Institute I have had the occasion to travel around the world and speak with religious leaders in scores of countries from across the ecumenical spectrum, and I find that many of them, while well-meaning and motivated by a deep love for God and humanity, simply do not have the faintest notion of the vital role of ethical business enterprise and entrepreneurial creativity for a flourishing economy that can lift people out of poverty. I do not say I am surprised by this fact. It is the reason the Acton Institute was founded in the first place, some twenty-two years ago.

Having been a pastor myself, I understand how easy it is to make the fixed-pie mistake of the offering plate, which is all about transferring wealth without asking how it is created in the first place. But it is a mistake, nonetheless, to think of wealth as if there were a static quantity of it, and redistribution were the answer to poverty. There is no good reason that the gap in understanding should persist between the entrepreneurial mindset, which is distinguished by its creativity, willingness to risk, and insight, and the pastoral-religious frame of reference, with its priority of tending to the needs of the most vulnerable out of the love with which God has first loved us. The approaches are complementary, not adversarial, for it is precisely those societies that have liberated the entrepreneur to create new wealth that have generated the reserves of wealth, along with the means of creating and delivering a host of positive goods and services, that have done the most to roll back extreme poverty and place people on the path to economic well-being.

Does the very prosperity that has lifted so many people out of extreme poverty also come with dangers? Undoubtedly. In a trenchant analysis of the free society, the economist Friedrich Hayek speculated, "It may be that a free society as we have known it carries in itself the forces of its own destruction, and that once freedom is achieved it is taken for granted and ceases to be valued." He goes on to ask, "Does this mean that freedom is valued only when it is lost, that the world must everywhere go through a dark phase of socialist totalitarianism before the forces of freedom can gather strength anew?"

He answers, "It may be so, but I hope it need not be."

Hayek offers what I consider a partial remedy to this threat: "We must be able to offer a new liberal program which appeals to the imagination. We must make the building of a free society once more an intellectual adventure, a deed of courage."[9] He is right, but I would add something: we must make the building of the free and virtuous society once more a *moral* adventure—for its construction was morally inspired in the first place. It emerged from an exalted vision of man and his inherent and transcendent destiny.

In his essay "The Weight of Glory," C. S. Lewis offers an evocative articulation of the anthropology—the understanding of man—I have in mind. "You have never talked to a mere mortal," he writes. "Nations, cultures, arts, civilizations—these are mortal, and their life is to ours as the life of a gnat. But it is immortals whom we joke with, work with, marry, snub, and exploit—immortal horrors or everlasting splendours."[10]

Such an understanding of the ultimate destiny of man is crucial to a free and virtuous society. We must continue to point out the utility of economic freedom—the undeniable fact that a free economy is the way to prosperity. But if we are concerned about the end of freedom in America and in our world, the decline and possible death of liberty and justice for all, then we would do well to remember the other "end" of freedom, the purpose and destiny of men and women called by their creator to lives of liberty and virtue. In the final analysis, very few people will go to the barricades to defend a system's utility. But a way of life that protects all that we hold dear, a civilization that elevates our spirits, a culture that is rooted in realities of eternal significance; this is a different story. For such a moral crusade, we will be able to raise a vast army.

Suggestions for Further Reading

Pope Benedict XVI, *Caritas in Veritate* (2009), available online at http://www.vatican.va/holy_father/benedict_xvi/encyclicals/documents/hf_ben-xvi_enc_20090629_caritas-in-veritate_en.html.

Samuel Gregg, *On Ordered Liberty: A Treatise on the Free Society* (Lexington, 2003).

Russell Hittinger, *The First Grace: Rediscovering the Natural Law in a Post-Christian World* (ISI Books, 2007).

Robert A. Sirico, *Toward a Free and Virtuous Society* (Acton Institute, 1997).

Thomas Williams, *Who is My Neighbor: Personalism and the Foundations of Human Rights* (Catholic University of America Press, 2005).

Afterword

In the previous pages I have attempted to sum up in an accessible manner a wide range of encounters, stories, ideas, and sources that have enabled me to see that there was at the beginning a natural truth embedded at the core of things, a harmony in the universe that holds if we do not rend asunder, by force, sin, or blind prejudice, the coherence which is ours naturally and which we all seek. I have done so at a very critical moment in history, when a loss of meaning and coherence in life—a degradation in our understanding of freedom—permeates society.

Where I have cast socialism, liberalism, collectivism, and central planning in a dark light, I mean no personal insult to those honest men and women who hold to those ideas. It has long been my belief that while we must be ruthless in pursuing the truth of ideas unswervingly, we must always remain gentle and respectful with the people with whom we disagree. This is not so easy a virtue to embrace in the heat of rhetorical battle. But in the last analysis, the dignity that human beings possess, which establishes their right to be free, abides as well in those with whom we disagree and whom we believe to be wrong. Being from Brooklyn—

a place not generally known for diplomacy—I find that I fail to put this principle into practice as often as I should. To the extent that at any point herein—or in any of my writings or public discourse—I have once again failed in this regard, I offer my most sincere *mea culpa*.

Not being a member of any political party, I confess to being dissatisfied in general with the pigeonholes and polarized language of "left and right" in economic, political, and philosophical conversation, and most frustratingly (and misleadingly) in religious discourse, which is the fashion of the day. In the formulation of my ideas and in my search for the truth, I attempt to think outside those boundaries, and I would like to think that anyone not knowing me personally and looking through my personal library in order to gauge where I am on the political spectrum would be perplexed. Still, to engage in discussion in a contemporary and comprehensible way, it is sometimes necessary to use the current idiomatic shorthand to get to the point.

I would also like to make note of my use of the phrase "the Judeo-Christian tradition." This is my own tradition. It is also the tradition I know best, doctrinally and historically, and it goes without saying that I have a special appreciation for its social contributions and its theological truth claims (to which I've dedicated my life). At the same time, I do not mean to suggest that this tradition is the exclusive contributor to the development and maintenance of economic freedom. The trick, it seems to me, is to be able to identify on the one hand the unique and undeniable contribution that Judeo-Christian revelation and anthropology played in the institutional development of liberty in the world, and yet not to close the door on how the truths about human liberty can be understood—discernible as they are through the natural reason—in other philosophical or theological contexts. In the end, of course, that is not my task or competency. I leave that to others more qualified and knowledgeable about how this would play itself out in, for example, a Hindu or Islamic context.

Human nature, like truth itself, is universal; and freedom is for everyone. The globalization of the market economy and the dramatic rise in prosperity in civilizations all over the world illustrate the point. While I believe that Christianity contains the fullness of the truth about the human person, many other religious traditions contain truth that can serve as a basis for the essential appreciation of human dignity that is, can, and must be embedded and reflected in market institutions if they are to function well—if, indeed, the human person is to function well and flourish. Certainly many holy people have emerged from under the shadow of political and economic tyranny, but freedom has never flourished absent virtue and spiritual sustenance.

This book describes a spiritual odyssey that has some things in common with that of St. Augustine, whom I see as a model for my own journey back to the freedom of my spiritual home. I was riveted by his words in *The Confessions* when I first read them, convicted of the truth that all men have an interior knowledge of their origin, and that if they can but find it in themselves to acknowledge and embrace that origin, they may also discover their own *telos*, their purpose, their proper end—because this end and this origin are, in the end, one and the same. But Augustine put it better than I could, and so I close with his words:

Late have I loved you,
O Beauty so ancient and so new,
late have I loved you!
You were within me, but I was outside,
and it was there that I searched for you.
In my unloveliness I plunged into the lovely things which you created.
You were with me, but I was not with you.
Created things kept me from you;
yet if they had not been in you they would not have been at all.
You called, you shouted, and you broke through my deafness.
You flashed, you shone, and you dispelled my blindness.
You breathed your fragrance on me;
I drew in breath and now I pant for you.
I have tasted you, now I hunger and thirst for more.
You touched me, and I burned for your peace.[1]

Acknowledgments

Rumor has it that the writing of a book is a solitary process. It certainly is a personal one, but it is in no way an isolated experience. I have learned so much from so many divergent people over the course of my life, much of which went into the compilation of this book.

I acknowledge Fr. Fredric W. Schlatter, S.J.; Fr. (and later Cardinal) Avery Dulles, S.J.; Rocco Buttiglione; and Michael Novak. Each of these men taught me not so much what to think, as how to think. And Pope (now Blessed) John Paul the Great, who taught me and the world so much, both through his words and his life.

I wish to express my indebtedness to the entire staff of the Acton Institute, whose dedication to the cause of human freedom inspires me each day, and without whom the wide-ranging scope of our mission would be impossible. In particular I would like to express my gratitude to: Jonathan Witt, whose shaping of my words and arguments made them gleam; Kevin Schmiesing, whose masterful research abilities and editorial skills are as consistent as they are prolific; my personal assistant Katharine Harger, who in addition to putting her attention to detail to work in keeping an eye on ever-changing redactions of the manuscript—all the while raising her family—also employed that same talent to ensure I would show up at the right city with the right speech in hand; and to Holly Rowley, whose infectious joy and eagle eye are both Wonders of the World.

Sam Gregg is a renaissance man and a dear friend, and Jeff Tucker wins the prize for intellectual agility—combining a command of the details of Misesian praxeology with an expertise in Gregorian chant (go figure).

At Regnery Publishing, I thank Harry Crocker, Executive Editor—a demanding though likable taskmaster when it comes to deadlines—for urging me to write this book, and Elizabeth Kantor, an author in her own right, whose linguistic and editorial insights improved the manuscript, as well as Maria Ruhl and Caitlin Jones for their fine copyediting.

I am grateful additionally to my religious family, the Community of St. Philip Neri, for their long-suffering, not only for the time and energy this book required of me and thus of our community life, but for their usual forbearance and charity. And to Theophilus, our dog, who acted as my muse by sitting (and most often napping) on the chair next to my desk, offering his own discrete critiques. To all of these and many more I owe a great debt, even if I stand alone in responsibility for the final text.

Notes

Introduction

1. International Monetary Fund, "A History of World Debt: How public debt has changed since 1880," *Finance & Development*, March 2011, available online at http://www.imf.org/external/pubs/ft/fandd/2011/03/pdf/picture.pdf.

Chapter One

1. Lord Acton, "The History of Freedom in Antiquity," *Selected Writings of Lord Acton*, vol. 1, *Essays in the History of Liberty*, ed. J. Rufus Fears (Liberty Fund, 1985), 5.

Chapter Two

1. The Constitution of the U.S.S.R., part 1: Declaration, January 31, 1924, available online at www.answers.com/topic/1924-constitution-of-the-ussr.

2. John Adams, "Message to the Officers of the First Brigade of the Third Division of the Militia of Massachusetts," October 11, 1798, *The Works of John Adams, Second President of the United States*, vol. 9 (Little, Brown, and Company, 1854), 229.
3. Alexis de Tocqueville, "Journey to England (1835)," in *Journeys to England and Ireland*, ed. Jacob Peter Mayer (Transaction Publishers, 1979), 117.
4. In the writing of this section the author wishes to acknowledge his indebtedness to Jean-Yves Calvez, S.J., and Jacques Perrin, S.J., *The Church and Social Justice: The Social Teaching of the Popes from Leo XIII to Pius XII* (Henry Regnery Company, 1961), 191 ff.
5. Thomas Aquinas discusses this in *Summa Theologica*, II-II, q. 66, a. 7.
6. The interview segment appears in the Acton Institute's PovertyCure DVD series, Session 3. Stark makes the point at greater length in *The Victory of Reason* (Random House, 2005), 71–72. The historian he alludes to in the interview, and directly quotes in the book, is Winwood Reade. The quotation is from *The Martyrdom of Man* (Watts, 1925), 108.
7. See Leonard Leo, "Opening remarks: 2010 Annual Report Rollout," 2010 U.S. Commission on International Religious Freedom by its chairman Leonard Leo, www.uscirf.gov/images/opening%20remarks%20leo.pdf.
8. William Bradford, *Of Plymouth Plantation*, 1620–1647, ed. Samuel Eliot Morison (Modern Library, 1967), in *The Founders' Constitution*, vol. 1 (University of Chicago Press, 1987), ch. 16, document 1 (1623), available online at http://press-pubs.uchicago.edu/founders/documents/v1ch16s1.html.
9. Odd Langholm, "Scholastic Economics," *Pre-Classical Economic Thought: From the Greeks to the Scottish Enlightenment*, ed. S. Todd Lowry (Kluwer Academic Publishers, 1987), 126–32.
10. For those interested in further study of the complicated history of usury, see *Sourcebook in Late-Scholastic Monetary Theory: The Contributions of Martin de Azpilcueta, Luis de Molina, S.J., and Juan de Mariana, S.J.*, ed. Stephen J. Grabill (Lexington Books, 2007).
11. See NIV Stewardship Study Bible (Zondervan, 2009), 244.
12. "Freddie Mac," Business Day section, *New York Times* online, updated February 28, 2012, http://topics.nytimes.com/top/news/business/companies/freddie_mac/index.html.

Chapter Three

1. Based on World Bank figures as analyzed in Daniel Griswold, *Mad About Trade: Why Main Street America Should Embrace Globalization* (Cato Institute, 2009), 127. The World Bank defines "absolute poverty" as living on less than 1.25 U.S. dollars per day. Here I use "abject" or "dire" poverty as synonymous with the World Bank's "absolute poverty." Fifty-two percent of the world's population lived in absolute poverty in 1981; by 2005, 25 percent did.
2. Peter Bauer, *Dissent on Development: Revised Edition* (Harvard University Press, 1971, 1979), 115.
3. Interview with President Paul Kagame in Kigali, Rwanda, PovertyCure, November 30, 2007, http://www.povertycure.org/voices/president-paul-kagame/#paul-kagame-the-entrepreneur-president.
4. Daniel Córdova, "Defeating Poverty Doing Business: The Case of the Flores Family and Topy Top," in *Lessons from the Poor: Triumph of the Entrepreneurial Spirit*, ed. Alvaro Vargas Llosa (Independent Institute, 2008), 55–120.
5. Hernando de Soto, *The Mystery of Capital* (Basic Books, 2000), 190.
6. This segment of her interview is featured in Acton Media's DVD Series on global poverty, scheduled for release in the second half of 2012.
7. See their website for more information at www.enersahaiti.com.
8. Quoted testimony begins at minute 59 of the March 10, 2010, U.S. Senate Committee on Foreign Relations hearing, available on the Committee website at http://www.foreign.senate.gov/hearings/building-on-success-new-directions-in-global-health.
9. Timothy T. Schwartz, *Travesty in Haiti* (BookSurge Publishing, 2008). See also Brian Reidl, "Another Year at the Federal Trough: Farm Subsidies for the Rich, Famous, and Elected Jumped Again in 2002," Heritage Foundation Backgrounder no.1763, May 24, 2004, www.heritage.org/research/reports/2004/05/another-year-at-the-federal-trough-farm-subsidies-for-the-rich-famous-and-elected-jumped-again-in-2002, and Ivan Roberts and Frank Jotzo, "2002 U.S. Farm Bill: Support and Agricultural Trade," ABARE Research Report 01.13, http://143.188.17.20/data/warehouse/pe_abarebrs99000755/PC12270.pdf.
10. See the archived USAID webpage "Direct Economic Benefits of U.S. Assistance by State," WaybackMachine, http://web.archive.org/

web/20010501044206/http://www.usaid.gov/procurement_bus_opp/states/. USAID has recently adopted new protocols allowing them to contract with local businesses in developing countries. See Federal Register vol. 77, no. 6, January 10, 2012, http://www.gpo.gov/fdsys/pkg/FR-2012-01-10/html/2011-33240.htm. A February 6, 2012, news story by Claire Provost in the *Guardian* described the change: "USAid now free to buy goods from companies in poor countries," http://www.guardian.co.uk/global-development/2012/feb/06/usaid-changes-procurement-policy. But Timothy Schwartz (*Travesty in Haiti*) notes that Western aid organizations have a long track record of promising reform to no avail. As of the writing of this chapter, it remains to be seen whether USAID's directive will materialize into a substantive step in the right direction.

11. See "Ease of doing business index (1=most business-friendly regulations," the World Bank, http://data.worldbank.org/indicator/IC.BUS.EASE.XQ?order=wbapi_data_value_2011+wbapi_data_value+wbapi_data_value-last&sort=asc.
12. "One possible approach to development aid would be to apply effectively what is known as fiscal subsidiarity, allowing citizens to decide how to allocate a portion of the taxes they pay to the State. Provided it does not degenerate into the promotion of special interests, this can help to stimulate forms of welfare solidarity from below, with obvious benefits in the area of solidarity for development as well." Pope Benedict XVI, *Caritas in Veritate*, 2009, no. 60, available online at http://www.vatican.va/holy_father/benedict_xvi/encyclicals/documents/hf_ben-xvi_enc_20090629_caritas-in-veritate_en.html.
13. Interview with Herman Chinery-Hesse in Ghana, July 28, 2010, available on YouTube, http://www.youtube.com/watch?v=bs9cJEE-G9c&list=UUJJniHyad24Lox_ioZVJfPA&index=29&feature=plcp. These and other quotations about poverty, aid, and development can be found at www.povertycure.org.
14. Moses Maimonides, Central Conference of American Rabbis, "Afternoon Service for Atonement Day" XIX (From Maimonides)," in *The Union Prayer Book for Jewish Worship*, vol.2 (Central Conference of American Rabbis, 1922), 300, http://ia600309.us.archive.org/4/items/unionprayerbookf02centuoft/unionprayerbookf02centuoft.pdf.
15. C. Neal Johnson, see "C. Neal Johnson on the Impact of a Job" on the Social Business section under the Issues tab of the PovertyCure website, http://www.povertycure.org/issues/social-business.

Chapter Four

1. Edmund A. Opitz, *Religion and Capitalism: Allies, Not Enemies* (Arlington House, 1970), 80.
2. Theodore Dalrymple, "What the New Atheists Don't See," *City Journal*, Autumn 2007, available online at http://www.city-journal.org/html/17_4_oh_to_be.html.
3. Matthew Parris, "As an atheist, I truly believe Africa needs God," A Faith to Live By blog by Neil Powell, February 18, 2011, available online at http://www.afaithtoliveby.com/2011/02/18/as-an-atheist-i-truly-believe-africa-needs-god/.

Chapter Five

1. Ludwig von Mises, "Profit and Loss," *Planning for Freedom* (Libertarian Press, 1952), 120.
2. See, for example, Todd Zywicki, "The Auto Bailout and the Rule of Law," *National Affairs* 7 (Spring 2011): 66–80, available online at http://www.nationalaffairs.com/publications/detail/the-auto-bailout-and-the-rule-of-law.
3. Mark J. Perry, "Q1: Exxon Paid Almost $1M per Hour in Income Taxes and Its Effective Tax Rate was 42.3%," Carpe Diem blog, April 28, 2011, available online at mjperry.blogspot.com/2011/04/exxonmobil-paid-almost-1m-per-hr-in.html, citing figures from Yahoo!Finance, see http://biz.yahoo.com/p/sum_qpmd.html. Eleven months later, as of March 16, 2012, the profit margin for the sector was 7.90 percent, higher but still well below that of dozens of other industries.
4. Francis de Sales, *Introduction to the Devout Life* (Doubleday, 1950), 164.
5. Ayn Rand, *The Virtue of Selfishness* (New American Library, 1964), 44.
6. Karl Marx, *The Communist Manifesto* (Penguin, 1967), 105.
7. John Larrivee summarizes well the moral damage done by communism in "It's Not the Markets, It's the Morals," in *Back on the Road to Serfdom: The Resurgence of Statism*, ed. Thomas E. Woods Jr. (ISI Books, 2010).

Chapter Six

1. These estimates are based on statistics from *Global Wealth Report 2011* (Credit Suisse Research Institute, 2011). Total wealth of the richest

1 percent in the world is 89 trillion USD, divided by a total world population of 7 billion.

2. Barnaby J. Feder, "COMPANY NEWS: Ben Leaving as Ben & Jerry's Chief," *New York Times*, June 14, 1994, available online at www.nytimes.com/1994/06/14/business/company-news-ben-leaving-as-ben-jerry-s-chief.html?pagewanted=all&src=pm.
3. National Conference of Catholic Bishops, *Economic Justice for All: Pastoral Letter on Catholic Social Teaching and the U.S. Economy* (National Conference of Catholic Bishops, 1986), no. 319. I and others had many problems with the document because of its repeated reference to the federal government as the chief means to supply society's needs—but at least its focus was on the poorest.
4. John Paul II, *Sollicitudo Rei Socialis*, encyclical letter for the twentieth anniversary of *Populorum Progressio*, December 30, 1987, no. 15, available online at http://www.vatican.va/holy_father/john_paul_ii/encyclicals/documents/hf_jp-ii_enc_30121987_sollicitudo-rei-socialis_en.html. In writing these words, the pope was echoing the vision of the Second Vatican Council's document *Gaudium et Spes*: "Since property and other forms of private ownership of external goods contribute to the expression of the personality, and since, moreover, they furnish one an occasion to exercise his function in society and in the economy, it is very important that the access of both individuals and communities to some ownership of external goods be fostered. Private property or some ownership of external goods confers on everyone a sphere wholly necessary for the autonomy of the person and the family, and it should be regarded as an extension of human freedom."
5. See chapter 5 of Arthur Brooks's *Gross National Happiness* (Basic Books, 2008) and chapters 3 and 4 of Brooks's *The Battle: How the Fight between Free Enterprise and Big Government Will Shape America's Future* (Basic Books, 2010).

Chapter Seven

1. Pope Benedict XVI, Encyclical Letter *Deus Caritas* Est, 2005, no. 26b, http://www.vatican.va/holy_father/benedict_xvi/encyclicals/documents/hf_ben-xvi_enc_20051225_deus-caritas-est_en.html.
2. Quoted in Michael B. Katz, *In the Shadow of the Poorhouse: A Social History of Welfare in America* (Basic Books, 1986), 154. It is important

to note that progressives such as Halbert, far from being Marxists, considered themselves to be working against the advance of radicalism by addressing the needs of the poor in an efficient, scientific fashion. The point here is that progressives shared with Marxists a disdain for the older, often religiously inspired methods of charitable assistance.

3. The "crowding out" of private charity by public (government) assistance is a phenomenon well known to public policy economists. See, for example, Russell Roberts, "A Positive Model of Private Charity and Public Transfers," *Journal of Political Economy* 92 (February 1984): 136–48.
4. Gary Bauer, "BAUER: Ending Welfare Reform," *Washington Times*, February 26, 2010, http://www.washingtontimes.com/news/2010/feb/26/ending-welfare-reform-as-we-know-it/?page=all.
5. Stewart E. Tolnay, *The Bottom Rung: African American Family Life on Southern Farms* (University of Illinois Press, 1999), 176.
6. Elijah Anderson, *Young Unwed Fathers: Changing Roles and Emerging Policies* (Temple University Press, 1994), 85. See also Mickey Hepner and W. Robert Reed, "The Effect of Welfare on Work and Marriage: A View from the States," *Cato Journal* 24 (Fall 2004), 349–70, and Robert Rector, *Marriage: America's Greatest Weapon Against Child Poverty*. Heritage Foundation Backgrounder #2465, September 16, 2010, available online at www.heritage.org/research/reports/2010/09/marriage-america-s-greatest-weapon-against-child-poverty.
7. Marvin Olasky, *The Tragedy of American Compassion* (Regnery, 1992), 113.
8. C. S. Lewis, *The Weight of Glory* (HarperOne, 2001), 46. Preached originally as a sermon in the Church of St. Mary the Virgin, Oxford, on June 8, 1942.
9. Thomas C. Reeves, *The Empty Church: Does Organized Religion Matter Anymore?* (Touchstone, 1996), 11.
10. There is debate about Mass attendance figures, but these are based on the available evidence. See "Sunday Morning: Deconstructing Catholic Mass Attendance in the 1950s and now," Nineteen Sixty-four blog, Center for Applied Research in the Apostolate, March 21, 2011, http://nineteensixty-four.blogspot.com/2011/03/sunday-morning-deconstructing-catholic.html. On ex-Catholics, see "Summary of Key Findings," Pew Forum on Religion and Public Life U.S. Religious Landscape Survey, 2007, at religions.pewforum.org/reports.
11. For one compelling argument connecting moral institutions (in particular the family) with economic well-being and government expansion, see

Jennifer Roback Morse, *Love and Economics: Why the Laissez-Faire Family Doesn't Work* (Spence, 2001). The Heritage Foundaton's Family Fact.org website tracks studies demonstrating the connections among religious practice, family life, and socio-economic well-being.

12. "Two in Five Single-Mother Families Are Poor," FamilyFacts.org, graph using data from the U.S. Census Bureau, Current Population Survey, 2011, http://www.familyfacts.org/charts/327/two-in-five-single-mother-families-are-poor.
13. The *Compendium of the Social Doctrine of the Church* (Pontifical Council for Justice and Peace, 2005), available at http://www.vatican.va/roman_curia/pontifical_councils/justpeace/documents/rc_pc_justpeace_doc_20060526_compendio-dott-soc_en.html, describes subsidiarity thus:

> *On the basis of this principle, all societies of a superior order must adopt attitudes of help (*"subsidium"*)—therefore of support, promotion, development—with respect to lower-order societies.* In this way, intermediate social entities can properly perform the functions that fall to them without being required to hand them over unjustly to other social entities of a higher level, by which they would end up being absorbed and substituted, in the end seeing themselves denied their dignity and essential place.
>
> Subsidiarity, understood *in the positive sense* as economic, institutional or juridical assistance offered to lesser social entities, entails a corresponding series of *negative* implications that require the State to refrain from anything that would de facto restrict the existential space of the smaller essential cells of society. Their initiative, freedom and responsibility must not be supplanted. (no. 186)

Although the concept is not exactly parallel, *sphere sovereignty*—a key notion in Protestant social thought—displays similar concern for the preservation of distinct roles for society's various institutions. Sphere sovereignty was articulated by the great Reformed thinker and statesman, Abraham Kuyper. Peter Heslam summarizes Kuyper's idea:

> For Kuyper, society was made up of a variety of spheres, such as the family, business, science, and art. They derived their authority not from the State, which occupied a sphere of its own, but from

God, to whom they are directly accountable. Each of the spheres developed spontaneously and organically, according to the powers God had given them in the first moments of creation. (Peter Heslam, "Prophet of a Third Way: The Shape of Kuyper's Socio-Political Vision," *Journal of Markets & Morality* 5 (Spring 2002): 17.)

14. Alexis de Tocqueville, *Democracy in America (1835, 1840)*, Book II, chapter 5, trans. Gerald E. Bevan (Penguin, 2003).
15. Marvin Olasky, *The Tragedy of American Compassion* (Regnery, 1992).
16. II Thessalonians 3:10.
17. I Timothy 5:9-14.

Chapter Eight

1. The Henry J. Kaiser Family Foundation, "Health Care Spending in the United States and Selected OECD Countries," Snapshots: Health Care Costs, April 2011, available online at http://www.kff.org/insurance/snapshot/oecd042111.cfm. For the more recent percentage of GDP going to health care and the forecast, see United Press International, Inc., "Healthcare costs to jump faster than GDP," Business News, July 28, 2011, available online at http://www.upi.com/Business_News/2011/07/28/Healthcare-costs-to-jump-faster-than-GDP/UPI-19251311884095/.
2. Wilhelm Röpke, *A Humane Economy*, 3rd ed. (ISI,1998), 150.
3. Kelly Kennedy, "Health care costs vary widely," *USA Today*, June 30, 2011, available online at http://www.usatoday.com/money/industries/health/2011-06-30-health-costs-wide-differences-locally_n.htm.
4. "Planning in the specific sense in which the term is used in contemporary controversy necessarily means central planning—direction of the whole economic system according to one unified plan. Competition, on the other hand, means decentralized planning by many separate persons." Friedrich A. Hayek, "The Use of Knowledge in Society," *American Economic Review*, XXXV no. 4 (American Economic Association, 1945), 519–30, available online at http://www.econlib.org/library/Essays/hykKnw1.html.
5. David Goldhill, "How American Health Care Killed My Father," *Atlantic*, September 2009, available online at http://www.theatlantic.com/magazine/archive/2009/09/how-american-health-care-killed-my-father/7617/.

6. "Nielsen Study Shows DVD Players Surpass VCRs," PRNewswire, www.prnewswire.com/news-releases/nielsen-study-shows-dvd-players-surpass-vcrs-57201447.html.
7. Steven H. Woolf, "The Power of Prevention and What it Requires," *Journal of the American Medical Association* 299 (May 28, 2008), 2437–9.
8. A. A. Hedley, et al., "Prevalence of Overweight and Obesity among U.S. Children, Adolescents, and Adults, 1999–2002," *Journal of the American Medical Association* 291 (June 16, 2004), 2847–50.
9. Edward J. Sondik, *Health, United States, 2007*, National Center for Health Statistics, Hyattsville, Maryland, www.cdc.gov/nchs/data/hus/hus07.pdf#fig01.
10. Donald Condit, *A Prescription for Health Care Reform* (Acton Institute, 2011). The monograph is available online here: https://www.smashwords.com/books/view/37582.
11. Rodney Stark, *The Rise of Christianity* (Princeton University Press, 1996), 82–3. Stark quotes Dionysius, "Festival Letters," as quoted in Eusebius, *The History of the Church*, bk 7, chapter 22 (Penguin, 1965 ed.), 237. The author wishes to express his appreciation to Michael Donald for pointing out this reference.
12. Guenter B. Risse, *Mending Bodies, Saving Souls: A History of Hospitals* (Oxford University Press, 1999), 73.
13. James Edward McClellen and Harold Dorn, *Science and Technology in World History: An Introduction* (Johns Hopkins University Press), 99 and 101.
14. "Faith-based organizations play a major role in HIV/AIDS care and treatment in sub-Saharan Africa," World Health Organization, February 8, 2007, http://www.who.int/mediacentre/news/notes/2007/np05/en/index.html.

Chapter Nine

1. A shocking instance of an otherwise mainstream environmental scientist seemingly fantasizing about a virus wiping out most of humanity is related by Forrest Mims, "Meeting Doctor Doom," *Citizen Scientist* (March 31, 2006), available on Infowars.com, http://www.infowars.com/articles/life/population_reduction_mims_responds_pianka.htm. For more sources and discussion of the controversy, see Jay W. Richards, *Money, Greed, and*

God: Why Capitalism Is the Solution and Not the Problem (HarperOne, 2009), 204 and 250 (endnote 33).

2. Alfred Lord Tennyson, *In Memoriam A.H.H.*, part 56, line 15.
3. Lynn White Jr., "The Historical Roots of Our Ecologic Crisis," *Science*, March 1967, 1203–7, available on EarthTalk Today, http://www.earthtalktoday.tv/earthtalk-voices/historical-roots-ecological-crisis.html.
4. See E. Calvin Beisner, *Where Garden Meets Wilderness: Evangelical Entry into the Environmental Debate* (Eerdmans, 1997).
5. Wesley Granberg-Michaelson, ed., *Tending the Garden: Essays on the Gospel and the Earth* (Eerdmans, 1987); Calvin B. DeWitt, ed., *The Environment and the Christian* (Baker, 1991); Calvin B. DeWitt, ed., *Missionary Earthkeeping* (Mercer University Press, 1993).
6. Augustine, *City of God*, book 1, Chapter 20.
7. Nicolaus Copernicus, *On the Revolutions of the Heavenly Spheres, Preface and Book I*, trans. John F. Dobson and Selig Brodetsky (1947), 149–73; Milton Munitz, ed., *Theories of the Universe: From Babylonian Myth to Modern Science* (Simon & Schuster, 1965).
8. Terry L. Anderson and Donald R. Leal, *Free Market Environmentalism*, rev. ed. (Palgrave, 2001), chapter 5.
9. This phenomenon was confirmed by a path-breaking study in the 1990s. Gene M. Grossman and Alan B. Krueger, "Economic Growth and the Environment," *Quarterly Journal of Economics* 110 (May 1995), pp. 353–77. "We find no evidence that environmental quality deteriorates steadily with economic growth. Rather, for most indicators, economic growth brings an initial phase of deterioration followed by a subsequent phase of improvement." Grossman and Krueger located the turning point from environmental degradation to improvement at approximately U.S. $8000 per capita.
10. The quotation is from page 195 of the second edition (Copyright 1810), available for electronic search at Google Books, http://books.google.com/books?id=rAYAAAAAQAAJ&printsec=frontcover&source=gbs_ge_summary_r&cad=0#v=onepage&q&f=false (Accessed March 18, 2012).
11. W. Stanley Jevons, *The Coal Question: An Inquiry Concerning the Progress of the Nation, and the Probable Exhaustion of Our Coal-Mines* (MacMillan and Co., 1865), xiii.
12. Walter E. Williams, "Environmentalists' Wild Predictions," *Townhall*, May 7, 2008, http://townhall.com/columnists/walterewilliams/2008/05/07/environmentalists_wild_predictions/page/full/. Williams's essay lists many other wildly wrong doomsday predictions by environmentalists.

13. Williams, "Environmentalists' Wild Predictions."
14. Quoted in Bernard Dixon, *What is Science For?* (Harper & Row, 1973), 198.
15. Paul Ehrlich, *The Population Bomb* (Ballantine Books, 1968), prologue.
16. Julian L. Simon, *The Ultimate Resource 2* (Princeton University Press, 1996), 35–36.
17. On elephants, see "Using Market Incentives to Save the Elephants," Community Markets for Conservation, 2010, http://www.itswild.org/market-incentives-to-save-elephants. On tigers, see Michael 't Sas-Rolfes, "Who Will Save the Tiger?" PERC Policy Series, PS–12, February 1998, http://www.perc.org/files/ps12.pdf.
18. Richard L. Stroup, "Endangered Species Act: Making Innocent Species the Enemy," PERC Policy Series, PS–3, April 1995, http://www.perc.org/articles/article648.php.

Chapter Ten

1. Arthur Brooks, *Gross National Happiness* (Basic Books, 2008). See in particular chapter 5, "Does Money Buy Happiness?"
2. John Dalberg-Acton, *Selected Writings of Lord Acton*, vol.3, *Essays in Religion, Politics, and Morality*, ed. J. R. Fears, (Liberty Classics, 1988), 613.
3. Mother Teresa, *No Greater Love*, ed. Becky Benenate and Joseph Durepos (New World Library, 1989), 97–98.
4. Alexis de Tocqueville, *Democracy in America* (1835, 1840), trans. Gerald E. Bevan (Penguin, 2003), 805–6.
5. Pope Paul VI, "Pastoral Constitution on the Church in the Modern World: *Gaudium et Spes*," December 7, 1965, no. 39, available online at http://www.vatican.va/archive/hist_councils/ii_vatican_council/documents/vat-ii_cons_19651207_gaudium-et-spes_en.html. The passage in full:

> We do not know the time for the consummation of the earth and of humanity, nor do we know how all things will be transformed. As deformed by sin, the shape of this world will pass away; but we are taught that God is preparing a new dwelling place and a new earth where justice will abide, and whose blessedness will answer and surpass all the longings for peace which spring up in the human heart. Then, with death overcome, the sons of God

will be raised up in Christ, and what was sown in weakness and corruption will be invested with incorruptibility. Enduring with charity and its fruits, all that creation which God made on man's account will be unchained from the bondage of vanity.

Therefore, while we are warned that it profits a man nothing if he gain the whole world and lose himself, the expectation of a new earth must not weaken but rather stimulate our concern for cultivating this one. For here grows the body of a new human family, a body which even now is able to give some kind of foreshadowing of the new age.

Hence, while earthly progress must be carefully distinguished from the growth of Christ's kingdom, to the extent that the former can contribute to the better ordering of human society, it is of vital concern to the Kingdom of God.

For after we have obeyed the Lord, and in His Spirit nurtured on earth the values of human dignity, brotherhood and freedom, and indeed all the good fruits of our nature and enterprise, we will find them again, but freed of stain, burnished and transfigured, when Christ hands over to the Father: "a kingdom eternal and universal, a kingdom of truth and life, of holiness and grace, of justice, love and peace." On this earth that Kingdom is already present in mystery. When the Lord returns it will be brought into full flower.

6. Dietrich Bonhoeffer, *Barcelona, Berlin, New York 1928–1931*, ed. Clifford J. Green, trans. Douglas W. Stott, volume 10, *Dietrich Bonhoeffer Works* (Fortress Press, 2008), 521.
7. G. K. Chesterton, *Orthodoxy* (Doubleday, 1990, original publication information: Dodd, Mead, and Co., 1908), 15. Chesterton was referring specifically to the doctrine of original sin.
8. James Madison, Federalist No. 51, available online at http://www.constitution.org/fed/federa51.htm.
9. Friedrich A. Hayek, "The Intellectuals and Socialism," *University of Chicago Law Review* (Spring 1949), available on the Ludwig von Mises Institute website at http://mises.org/daily/2984.
10. C. S. Lewis, *The Weight of Glory* (HarperOne, 2001), 46. Preached originally as a sermon in the Church of St. Mary the Virgin, Oxford on June 8, 1942.

Afterword

1. St. Augustine, *The Confessions*, bk. 10, ch. 27, paragraph 38, as used in the Roman Office of Readings for the Feast of Saint Augustine, August 28, *Liturgy of the Hours*, vol. 4 (Catholic Book Publishing Company, 1975), 1357.

Index

B

C

D

E

F

G

H

M

N

O

P

Q

R

S

Y

Z